TV News
Can It Be Trusted?

Ray Spangenburg and Kit Moser

Enslow Publishers, Inc.

40 Industrial Road   PO Box 38
Box 398   Aldershot
Berkeley Heights, NJ 07922   Hants GU12 6BP
USA   UK

http://www.enslow.com

In memory of Lloyd,
who knew what good journalism is

Copyright © 2003 by Ray Spangenburg and Kit Moser

All rights reserved.

No part of this book may be reproduced by any means without the written permission of the publisher.

Library of Congress Cataloging-in-Publication Data

Spangenburg, Ray, 1939-
    TV news : can it be trusted? / Ray Spangenburg and Kit Moser.
        p. cm. — (Issues in focus)
    Summary: Discusses what makes a story newsworthy, the different people who are part of television newscasts, the reliability and distortions of these broadcasts, and how to use critical thinking when watching the news.
    Includes bibliographical references and index.
      ISBN 0-7660-1942-X
    1. Television broadcasting of news—Juvenile literature.
    2. Television broadcasting of news—Objectivity—Juvenile literature.
    [1.Television broadcasting of news.] I. Title: Television news. II. Moser, Diane, 1944- III. Title. IV. Issues in focus (Hillside, N.J.)
    PN4784.T4 S68 2003
    070.1'95—dc21
                                            2002012523

Printed in the United States of America

10 9 8 7 6 5 4 3 2 1

To Our Readers:
We have done our best to make sure all Internet Addresses in this book were active and appropriate when we went to press. However, the author and the publisher have no control over and assume no liability for the material available on those Internet sites or on other Web sites they may link to. Any comments or suggestions can be sent by e-mail to comments@enslow.com or to the address on the back cover.

Illustration Credits: AP/Worldwide: pp. 21, 33, 86, 96; Corbis Images Royalty-Free: p. 50; Julian Hirshowitz/Corbis: p. 31; Huntington College: p. 79; Mark M. Lawrence Photography/Corbis: p. 14; National Archives: p. 11; Painet Images: pp. 8, 25, 39, 63, 82.

Cover Illustrations: Hemera Technologies (background); Corbis Images Royalty-Free (inset).

Contents

Prologue   5

1 Stay Tuned for the News   9

2 Inside TV News 27

3 Who Is Running the Show? 36

4 When Trust Is in Danger 56

5 Some Tricks of the Trade 77

6 Thinking Critically About
the News 89

Epilogue 99

Chapter Notes 103

Glossary 107

Further Reading 109

Internet Addresses 110

Index 111

Prologue

At 7:15 A.M., Pacific Daylight Time, the phone rang. It was early for a phone call—but since the authors of this book are a husband-and-wife writing team writing for eastern publishers, they knew it could be an editor from the East Coast. Because of the time difference, it was already 10:15 there. It was not an editor, though. It was their good friend Pat. "Turn on your TV," she said urgently. She sounded serious. "Did you hear what is happening in New York? Did you hear about the terrorism? And Washington, D.C.?"

The date was September 11, 2001.

The two writers had been working late the night before, so they were barely awake, much less checking the TV news. They switched it on. For the rest of the day, along with most Americans, they watched with horror as a story of destruction and terror unfolded on their television screen. By the time they first tuned in, two hijacked jet airliners had plowed into the Twin Towers of the World Trade Center in New York and a third had crashed into the Pentagon in Washington, D.C. Later, a fourth hijacked plane crashed in a Pennsylvania cornfield. Thousands of people were killed—people who were innocently going to work or riding on a plane on a beautifully clear September day.

The entire nation shuddered with those explosions. The tremors themselves did not reach California, of course. People in St. Louis, Missouri, could not smell the acrid smoke that billowed up from the fires. Many people in New York and Washington knew someone who died in these tragic events, but most people in the rest of the country did not. Yet everyone in the United States was connected to it—and many people in other countries felt their impact. How? For the most part, television news services. They had videos. They interviewed witnesses. They talked to people looking for loved ones who had gone to work that morning and had not come home. They discussed what was happening with experts from many fields.

Most of the networks obviously were making a big effort to keep the facts straight. The teams of news reporters, fact checkers, researchers, editors, and announcers worked around the clock to gather and verify accurate information.

Yet hundreds of factors influenced and altered what the networks broadcast. Everything was happening fast, and they were moving fast to keep up. They had a mission to fulfill: get the news and get it out. They wanted to bring new facts to their listeners as quickly as possible.

Of course, they also wanted to make sure not to lag behind the other news teams on competing networks and stations. Even in these tragic circumstances, they felt the pressures of needing to be first with what Americans wanted to hear and see. To do that, they had to move quickly—and sometimes they had to correct errors. Most of the news commentators remarked that they were trying to be as accurate as possible under the circumstances.

The events of September 11, 2001, tested the capabilities of news organizations the world over. Many rose to the occasion and provided a fabric of connection between the rest of the world and the most directly affected victims. They helped leaders and citizens worldwide recognize the magnitude of terrorism's threat to the peaceful lives of everyone. In a sad way, it brought Americans together in a common resolve to overcome the destruction wreaked by a handful of suicidal individuals. The TV news coverage showed all this, and it was TV news at its best.

Television news has both strengths and weaknesses. It is an important source of information. Many people depend on TV news for nearly all their information about their community, their state, their country, and the rest of the world. Because of the importance of TV news in most people's lives,

During and after the collapse of the World Trade Center on September 11, 2001, television news teams kept the world informed on a minute-by-minute basis.

everyone needs to know how many forces influence the news presentations we see on TV.

This book takes a look inside TV news coverage. It shows how the news is put together: how the news is gathered, who makes the decisions about what we see and hear, how presentation affects what we think we see. It also looks at the influences on the news: the power of sponsors, the importance of ratings, and the need to make profits.

Finally, this book talks about how to spot untruthfulness or half-truths in news presentations—and when to suspend judgment until further information is available.

1

Stay Tuned for the News

Today, television news brings events from all over the world right into nearly everyone's living room. It brings us more knowledge of faraway lands, people, and events than our ancestors ever experienced. Video footage taken on the spot makes grim happenings both real and vivid. On our TVs we have seen real battlegrounds, starving children, families of murder victims, and airplanes colliding with buildings. TV news also opens connections and understanding between people we have never met and whose states or countries we may never visit. For today's audiences, television news makes possible a breadth of knowledge and heightened awareness that would not otherwise be possible.

Who Needs News?

Information gives power to those who have it. The players on a basketball team cannot play the game successfully unless they know the rules. Students at school need to know where their classrooms are located, what day the big test will be, and what the dress code is. People in a community need to know what is happening around them. All of us need to know what is happening in the world. As a nation, or as individuals, we need to know about wars, accidents, triumphs for freedom, or dangers of oppression. We need to know how we can help and how we can protect ourselves. Everyone needs to know the news for survival. Ever since the days of the cave dwellers, people have needed to know what is going on around them. In today's complex world, information is the lifeblood of our society.

In more primitive times, the news traveled by drumbeat or smoke signals. Today, most people rely on the *media* (a means of mass communication, such as newspapers or television) for information beyond events in their immediate neighborhood. That is, they read newspapers and magazines, listen to radio, hook up to the Internet, and watch television. The leading news source for Americans, however, is TV news. According to a nationwide poll by the Media Studies Center at the University of Connecticut, 65 percent

Television news can keep the nation informed of important public events. This news team is filming the civil rights march on Washington, August 28, 1963.

of the 1,002 people interviewed January 11–18, 1999, said that television was their most important source of news.[1]

What Is "The News"?

News, according to one dictionary, is information "of sufficient interest or importance to the public to warrant reporting in the media."

How does one decide, though, what makes an item news? What makes it interesting or important to the public? Who makes that decision? Just putting it on a news program sometimes is all it takes. As Martin Mayer comments in his book, *Making the News*, "The act of broadcasting makes the event 'news.'"[2] That puts a lot of power in the hands of those who put together the news programs we watch. Sometimes they handle that power with a healthy sense of responsibility, as they did in the days following September 11, 2001. Sometimes, they may not.

Journalists and television executives alike tend to focus on the unusual. Thousands of airplanes take off and land safely every day—but safe takeoffs and landings are not news. They are normal events—the way things usually work. A crash is news. A hijacking is definitely news. An event as terrible as the events of September 11, 2001, is horrendous news. On that morning, four jetliners full of passengers were hijacked. All four were diverted from their intended routes. Three plowed into buildings full of people—two into the Twin Towers in New York City and one into the Pentagon in Washington, D.C. The fourth ended its flight in flames in a Pennsylvania cornfield. A group of passengers in the fourth jetliner overcame the hijackers and caused the plane to crash before it could reach the intended target. These events were covered as they happened by television news. As people watched in horror, thousands of questions came to their minds. Television news teams made a nonstop effort to explore the questions and present the stories with videotapes, recordings, interviews, and commentary.

No journalist had to stop to wonder whether this was news. They knew people would want to know what happened. People wanted to know the stories of the victims. They wanted to know who hijacked the airplanes and why. What happened on board? What happened to the people in the three buildings? They also needed to know whether it would be safe to fly again. Would it be safe to fly tomorrow? Would airports even be open? Television news teams and the experts and officials they interviewed tried to answer as many questions as they could, as quickly as they could.

With serious faces and genuine concern, the TV news team members showed an obvious effort to get the stories right. They also clearly felt the pressure to get their stories on the air quickly. Their audience was eager to know. Also, the news teams were all in competition with each other. Could they be completely accurate with so little time to check and recheck their facts? No, but most of them tried. They used phrases such as, "As far as we know . . ." to show the uncertainty of their information.

A firefighter stands among the rubble and ashes of the World Trade Center, which collapsed on September 11, 2001.

September 11, 2001, and its aftermath was far from a normal news story. What makes a set of facts, a story, or an event into news?

What Makes the News Really "News"?

To be counted as news, a story generally needs to pass one or more of the ten basic tests of newsworthiness: change (or suspense), disaster (or tragedy), the bizarre (or novel), timeliness, conflict (or controversy), human interest, impact, local interest, progress, and celebrity. Why? Stories with these attributes touch something human within us—the desire to be frightened, to experience change, to gain relief from boredom or feel warmth and caring, to obtain information about changes that affect our own lives, and to enjoy vicarious adventures through stars and celebrities.[3]

- **Change (or suspense).** A story without an ending—one for which the conclusion is unresolved—can hold public interest for a long time. People will tune in for an update, to hear the latest progress, especially if they expect a conclusion will come. On the day after the nation voted in the U.S. presidential election in 2000, the name of the winner was still unknown. Yet everyone wanted to hear the latest story about the recounts and the administrative decisions that would finally decide the outcome. The suspense was incredible, and it was very big news.

- **Disaster (or tragedy).** A ferry gets caught in a storm and sinks, killing five hundred people in the North Sea. A powerful earthquake causes bridges and freeways to collapse in San Francisco. A volcano erupts, spewing lava over city streets in Goma, Congo, forcing some 400,000 people from their homes. Terrorists crash planes into the World Trade Center and the Pentagon. These events are all very big news, and television's ability to bring on-the-spot film into people's living rooms makes this type of news one of the strongest for TV news. People care about stories like these.

- **The bizarre (or novel).** John B. Bogart, editor of the *New York Sun* in the late 1880s, once said, "When a dog bites a man, that is not news, because it happens so often. But if a man bites a dog, that is news."[4] If elements of the story are unique, unexpected, or novel, it may be news.

- **Timeliness.** News is not news unless it is new. The "breaking story," the story that is coming in right now, is definitely news. If people are saying, "Did you hear about . . ." then it is news.

- **Conflict (or controversy).** People taking sides, people at war, or people outraged at injustices (real or unreal)—these are conflicts that make news. Even family battles can be news. Animosity, hatred, and anger attract attention. Political arguments and fights between sports fans—conflicts great and small—all make for news.

- **Human interest.** A story filled with human emotion, warmth, and the ability to make eyes tear up always commands attention. A Cuban boy, Elián Gonzalez, fled Cuba by boat with his mother in November 1999 to join relatives in Florida. But the boat capsized, and his mother drowned. Elián, who arrived safely in Florida, then became the center of a tearful, emotional custody battle between his Florida relatives and his father, who wanted him back in Cuba. (The story had conflict, too.) What made the story news for months, though, was the fact that an innocent child was caught between adults—and the two nations, the United States and Cuba—who would decide his fate. This small boy's future became an international debate. Many people who had little interest in politics or immigration laws became caught up by this compelling human-interest story and were anxious to see how it would end. (Suspense was at play here, as well.)

- **Impact.** How many people are affected by the story? Thousands? If so, it is news. If every first grader in the nation is required to have a tetanus vaccination, that is news. A great many families are affected. (This news story would also be controversial, because not everyone would agree on whether this was a good policy or a bad policy.) Are the consequences of the story large? Do they have world significance? A firm peace pact between Israel and Palestine would certainly be big news.

- **Local interest.** Will a gigantic shopping center be built near the edge of town in Columbia, Missouri? For those who live in Columbia, this is a news story. For those living in nearby Mexico, Missouri, it may still be news, but less so. Do the people who live in Reno, Nevada, care about this question at all? Probably not. For them, it is too distant and has too little impact to be news.

- **Progress.** Everyone likes to think that some improvement, either small or large, is taking place. From new sidewalks or improved freeways to a better floorplan in the grocery store, from a remodeled skateboard ramp to new textbooks with better illustrations— improvement and progress bring a positive edge to a story. The more measurable the progress is, the more satisfying the story is. Maybe the world is not so bad after all. This may seem like a strange contrast with tragedy, disaster, conflict, and controversy, but people like this kind of news, too. (However, it would be interesting to test which kind of story seems more exciting and interesting to most people.)

- **Celebrity.** People love to know what movie stars are doing (especially if their doings are a little scandalous). They like to know what Prince Charles of England said about genetically engineered foods. They want to know what Britney Spears wore to the Grammy Awards. The thirst for knowledge about celebrities is insatiable. This is always news— maybe not in large doses for everyone (people do not always agree about which celebrity is the most interesting)—but celebrity comings and goings do have a high interest value.

Most TV news programs will have several of these kinds of stories, for variety. The more of these attributes a single story has, of course, the more strongly it appeals to people in the audience and the more different types of people it will interest. Take a look at a TV news program for yourself and see how many of these attributes you can spot in one program. Which ones seem strongest? How many can you identify in one program?

"Who, What, When, Where, Why, and How?"

Every new reporter and journalism student can cite the questions a news story must answer: "The five Ws (Who? What? When? Where? Why?) and How?" Unfortunately, in a TV news story that airs for only thirty seconds, reporters have little time to cover more than just those five basics. Sometimes they do not have time for even that. In a news program lasting only a half hour or an hour—minus time for commercials—no topic or story can receive more than a brief introduction. (One survey of a hundred newscasts reported that fifteen had more commercials than they had news, in terms of airtime.[5]) This is one of the biggest challenges faced by TV news programs.

In a healthy society, information must be freely available. It also must be trustworthy. Without these safeguards, the news can become propaganda (the deliberate spreading of ideas to damage or help a cause) all too easily. Yet, under the time shortages faced by television news teams, how can a news program provide enough information to be useful? Also, how can the information be trusted, given the time pressures under which programmers work?

As TV journalist Ted Koppel writes, electronic technologies are geared toward getting and delivering the news speedily. Speed, he explains, has always been important in the journalist's job. But in the past, the goal of speed has always been offset by another tradition: thoroughness. "Traditional journalism," Koppel writes, "requires a sorting out of good information from bad, of the important from the trivial. That sort of commitment and expertise may be out of fashion, but the need for it is greater than ever before."[6]

So, television news is faced with an almost impossible responsibility: to deliver reliable, accurate information day after day, while rushing toward screen time at breakneck speed. In today's electronic world, many of the processes of news gathering, photography, filming, and even writing are far more efficient than ever before. However, these advantages only set a greater expectation of immediate results.

Beyond these challenges, Koppel adds, there is another. "There are at least two kinds of extreme ignorance," he writes. "The first exists in a vacuum, where no information is available." Clearly, having no information can be dangerous. However, Koppel points out, a second kind of ignorance exists, when "a world of informational anarchy" overloads us

Journalists Ted Koppel and Barbara Walters posed for a picture in October 2000. Koppel has written about the importance of thinking critically about how the news is presented.

with so much information that the mind becomes confused and does not know what to believe. "We are drowning in information," he remarks, "and starving for knowledge." According to Koppel, this kind of information overload describes the world of the third millennium. "In such a world," he concludes, "there is more of a need for good journalism than ever before."[7]

The Importance of Trust

What exactly is "good journalism," though? Journalists, like doctors and other professionals, maintain a code of ethics, and the standards are high. Television journalists are no exception. The Radio-Television News Directors Association (RTNDA) states in the preamble of its Code of Ethics and Professional Conduct:

> Professional electronic journalists should operate as trustees of the public, seek the truth, report it fairly and with integrity and independence, and stand accountable for their actions.[8]

The code expands on all the major concepts mentioned in the preamble: public trust, truth, fairness, integrity, independence, and accountability.

- **Trust.** The code's central recognition of the need for public trust recognizes the journalist's key responsibility as a bearer of news. The public, or audience, must be able to rely on this person as honest and forthright.

- **Truth.** The journalist has a responsibility to seek out truth and avoid distorting what is true. Sources (where the information came from, or who provided it) should be stated clearly. Nothing presented should be misleading.

- **Fairness.** Reporting should be fair and balanced. Both sides of controversial questions should be presented, without bias (leaning one way or the other). Without fairness, news can easily become propaganda.

- **Integrity.** A journalist should never commit acts that cause questions about his or her integrity and decency, according to the code. This idea reinforces the need for clarity about sources. It establishes that nothing presented should be misleading. The journalist should clearly label opinions and commentary so the audience does not mistake one person's thoughts or feelings for facts.

- **Independence.** Journalists, the code says, need to function independently. They need to be able to report freely without fear of consequences and without expecting to gain favors.

- **Accountability.** Finally, journalists must be accountable. They must take responsibility for their actions and see themselves as accountable to the public, to their profession, and to themselves.[9]

Objective Reporting

Throughout this challenging code of ethics is a theme: Television news reporting—like all journalism—has a responsibility to report the news objectively. What is objective reporting? "Objective" means uninfluenced by personal opinions or prejudices—and being truly objective is much more difficult than most people think. Try describing a good friend or a family member or, even more difficult, someone who is mean, just by telling facts. It is important not to use words that carry loaded meanings or that express opinion or emotion. That is objective reporting. Now watch a TV news broadcast. Was the reporting objective? Can anyone really be objective?

It may be helpful to keep in mind that different types of journalism do not always have the same goals. However, none of those goals grant license to step aside from journalism's basic code of ethics, as outlined by the RTNDA.

For example, straight news reporting must always attempt to be strictly objective, unbiased, and balanced. A straight news story should not reflect the writer's or the producer's opinion. If a film clip shows an interview with a victim's mother, the coverage should also show another side of the story—perhaps an interview with a teacher or neighbor of the accused.

Other types of reporting—documentaries, interpretive pieces, and analytical discussions—follow their own rules about objectivity.

Documentary filming is fact-related, filming real people speaking spontaneously, without a script. It focuses on real events. However, a documentary is considered an art form and always reflects the opinions and vision of the filmmaker. The structure, the organization, and the timing are all in his or her hands during editing. This person is telling a story. Unlike real life, a documentary usually is fashioned to have a beginning, a middle, and an ending. We, the viewers, see the facts through the eyes of the filmmaker. Because documentaries are based on fact, many people think of them as news-based—and they are. Viewers can learn a great deal of information from a documentary. However, a documentary is also a good place to look for the ways people can cast facts in a rosy or a somber light, depending on their goals.

An interpretative piece is usually shorter and more tightly knit than a documentary. It may explore an idea or place a spotlight on an artist's work. For example, it might cover the opening of a new exhibit of the Georgia O'Keeffe Museum in Santa Fe, New Mexico. It might focus on a few pieces, discuss interpretations of her work, and possibly connect that

Television news reporters are expected to follow a code of ethical conduct that requires them to be truthful, fair, and responsible. Above is a news anchor in an Australian TV station.

with a few highlights about her life in nearby Taos. It expresses opinion—but it should be clear that the opinions do not reflect an unbiased view.

A strong and ethical analytical discussion would delve into causes and backgrounds behind a controversial issue. It should explore more than one side of the issue, and the presentations should be evenly balanced in strength. Ideally, any analysis should be given enough time for a reasonably thorough examination of the issue.

Inside
TV News

When someone wants to know what makes a car run, she looks under the hood. So, let us take a look inside a TV newsroom to see what makes a news program run—beginning with the people we usually see at the news desk as the opening credits roll by, the anchors.

The Anchor

An anchor is the host—the person or team of people everyone always refers to as the program unfolds: "Back to you, Donna." Or, "Back to you, Ted." The anchor provides the links between stories and "anchors" the program down. So, even though there is no relationship between the story about the air controllers' strike at the airport and all the stoplights being out downtown, the anchor might jokingly make a connection: " . . . and speaking of traffic control, there wasn't any downtown, either. Here's Sue with that story." In TV jargon, the anchors are known as the "talent" because their job is to be charming, speak in pleasant tones, and read clearly and smoothly from the teleprompter. The anchor may also need to think quickly and smooth over problems with links to field reporters or telephone interviews. Except for filler (such as small talk), most of what an anchor says is written by journalists before the program begins. Only in some very small local television stations do anchorpeople actually do any reporting legwork or write their own stories. Most anchorpeople are primarily newsreaders.

Covering Sports and Weather

In the studio family, the sports reporter usually plays the part of the eager-to-please juvenile. Almost always male, he jokes and banters, playing a subservient role to the anchors. Strangely, viewers seem to feel comfortable with this formula, even though many people take sports news very seriously.

The weather reporter, on the other hand, may be male or female. He or she may make light comments, but the weather news is serious business. Sometimes stations try to outdo each other with having the most certified meteorologists on staff and the most high-tech displays. Partly because TV news stations can provide satellite views of oncoming weather systems, they can play an important part in preparing a community for heavy or dangerous weather, such as a hurricane. This coverage can provide a real service to a community—offering warning and sound advice for an imminent storm. TV coverage can keep audiences advised about the location of the storm, its strength and the damage it has done so far, and when they can expect it to arrive. News teams typically pass on information from emergency management authorities, the American Red Cross, and other officials. They keep viewers informed about where they can get help and what they can do.

Field Correspondents

On-location reporting brings excitement and immediacy into the newsroom. The field correspondent is on the spot, watching the floodwaters rise, looking over the wreckage from an earthquake or storm. As rain pours down or a blizzard whips against the reporter's mittened hands, viewers feel that they are there too. Even if the field reporter is just standing outside the state capitol building to report on the deadlocked budget session, she brings viewers closer to the action.

This is where television news reporting excels. It can also be where inaccuracies creep in because the reporter cannot have a clear overview of what is happening in several places. He can only report on what is happening in his particular location. So he may be reporting on the crash of an airplane in a neighborhood of Queens, New York, as reporters did on November 12, 2001. She may be interviewing a man who lives next door to a house that was hit by part of the plane, and she can find out something about that man's experience—a very vivid and moving report. However, a reporter cannot know what is happening in other parts of the neighborhood where other parts of the plane have fallen. In a rapidly moving story, the on-location reporter has the "worm's-eye view," not the bird's-eye view.

Beyond the TV Screen

What the public does not see is the complex process that takes place behind the scenes to fill the seventeen total minutes of news that airs for each half hour of programming (after subtracting time given to commercial advertisements and "teases"—snippets of upcoming news stories).[1] The news director makes the important decision about what the lead story will be—the first story in a news program. Like the top front-page headline in a newspaper, this is the story the audience will perceive as the most important.

Producers—individuals who oversee all phases of the production process from filming to editing—also have a key role in this crucial decision. As the story develops, the producer decides what goes in and what stays out. She guides the work of reporters and photojournalists. Along the way, she makes hundreds of

On-location reporting brings the viewer to the scene of action.

decisions about how to develop the story. This individual, really, is the gatekeeper for the ethical standards of journalism. As veteran TV reporter and TV journalism instructor Valerie Hyman writes,

> It's hard to remain true to those principles in today's competitive environment. You may enter a newsroom that has chosen to do 'happy, warm, fuzzy' news, perhaps to the exclusion of important, albeit unpleasant, stories. Or your first job may put you in the swirling middle of a tabloid-style approach, emphasizing high story count, violence, and sex.[2]

Hyman sees the producer's job as keeping citizens informed—using the tools of "compelling material, presented in a form that makes sense, in a context that shows you understand not just what happened, but what it means."[3]

Once the stories are lined up, a team of writers, researchers, and video crews gather the news, under the direction of the producer. Interviews take place and may be filmed—either on location or in the studio. These sessions involve camera people, floor managers, sound technicians, makeup people, lighting technicians. Every second of airtime is managed carefully. Once the videotaping is done, the editing begins—and everything viewers see is shaped in this process. This is the final cut, determined by the producers and editors. Important information can either be lost here or placed in crisp focus. These decisions often have to be made very quickly, as airtime approaches. And the pressures to make money by boosting viewer ratings always loom behind every choice.

The TV News Consultant

It is the consultant's job to keep track of a TV station's ratings and to find the right personalities and tactics for the stations to use to help them achieve higher ratings. Sometimes, with a low-rated station, the consultant may make recommendations to change everything on the show completely, from the sets to the way the news is reported and the stories that are featured. Consultants may even suggest changes in the way the anchorpeople dress, wear their hair, or interact with one another. In her book *An Anchorwoman's Story*, former news anchor Christine Craft tells how the consultants hired by her television station, KMBC

Former news anchor Christine Craft was told she was "too old, too ugly," and "not deferential to men." She is shown here outside the Kansas City federal courthouse where she filed a lawsuit against her employer for removing her from her position as anchor.

in Kansas City, insisted that she change the color and length of her hair. They also told her to wear particular kinds and colors of dresses. She also said they often interrupted her work as she prepared for her news shows to demand that she try on various clothing combinations.

Another obvious problem, as Craft points out, is that consultants tend to apply what works on one station to all stations, thus making all newscasts look more or less alike. Sometimes, of course, this strategy does not work. A television personality who rates high because of his or her particular style in New York City or Chicago may play very poorly in Kansas City, Missouri, or Omaha, Nebraska. Also, a local personality from Omaha may fare poorly in news areas such as New York or Chicago, where viewers are surrounded by a different culture and have different expectations. Craft says she was told that her Kansas City viewers resented the occasional references she made on the news to her days working at a station in California. (Ironically, when she was first hired for the job, the station that hired her promoted her as being a top-flight, highly rated newscaster from California.)

Sometimes, on the consultant's advice, the station may replace anchors who "do not test well"— that is, those who receive negative reports on the basis of questions that the consultants ask of local news viewers. In Christine Craft's case, the research reports were disastrous. She recounts receiving the news:

"Christine, our viewer research results are in and they are really devastating. The people of Kansas City don't like watching you anchor the news because you are too old, too unattractive, and you are not sufficiently deferential to men. . . . When the people of Kansas City see your face, they turn the dial [change the channel]."[4]

The station took Craft off the anchor desk and assigned her to behind-the-scenes reporting, a decision she contested in court. The story illustrates the enormous impact ratings can make on television programming and specifically on the way the news is delivered and by whom.[5]

Today, a tightening economy has made inroads on the power of consultants in local TV stations. Still, in many locales they continue to have a big influence on what television viewers see on the local news.

3

Who Is Running the Show?

People sometimes forget that television programming—including television news—is for sale, in a way. Television stations and networks are businesses. Like any other business, they have to make a profit to keep going. So, television news programs are expected to bring in money, just the same as any other product. Owners, stockholders, and investors have provided the money to produce the programs, but they expect something in return. They provide those funds with the expectation that they will receive money back—a return on investment.

How can a news program make money? Anyone can plug a TV set into an outlet, turn it on, and watch the news. If the program is broadcast on the airwaves, the audience does not pay anything for the privilege of watching. So, most news programs on the airwaves—and even most transmitted by cable—make their money by selling time for commercials. The station or network sets aside segments of time to sell, and advertisers, or sponsors, buy time associated with a program.

The Path to Our Living Rooms

Initially, in the United States, television programming originated from one of three national broadcast networks or from local television stations. A local station was usually an affiliate of—that is, it was associated with—one of the networks. Today, those three broadcast networks—ABC (American Broadcasting Company), CBS (Columbia Broadcasting System) and NBC (National Broadcasting Company)—remain as giants in the industry. However, programs, and the signal that delivers them to the nation's living rooms, may come from several other sources.

In 1967, after the three commercial networks abandoned their public-service programming, a Carnegie Commission report recommended the establishment of a fourth, public television network. Several educational, nonprofit stations already existed throughout the United States. The new network, PBS (Public Broadcasting Service), would knit together these stations. The network was established by Congress in 1967. By 1998, it had grown to over three hundred stations. Its programming is created primarily by individual stations around the country, and some of it is purchased from Great Britain, especially from the BBC (British Broadcasting Corporation). The main difference between PBS and commercial networks is that public television is financed differently. Some support comes from the federal government, but that has lessened in recent years, since 1982. Some support comes from corporate sponsors, but there are no commercials. Most remaining support comes from memberships, or contributions from individual viewers.

Because its sponsorship is primarily the public, public television news is often considered more objective and less biased than news programs carried by the commercial networks. However, viewers should recognize that everyone has some biased views, and naturally an organization tries to protect its own existence. PBS may be just as likely as any other network to reflect the opinions of those who pay for the programming. It is just a different group from the sponsors of the commercial networks. PBS is supported by members who pledge money to support the programming. As a group, PBS subscribers tend to support the arts, have an academic background, and have liberal political leanings. PBS is unlikely to be any more eager to bite the hand that feeds it than any other network. So, PBS would be unlikely to air programs such as *The Jerry Springer Show*, a professional wrestling match, or a news segment contending that plastics make good landfill—none of which are likely to appeal to their members or their audience.

In the past decade, however, these two types of broadcast television transmission have become outstripped in numbers by cable and satellite networks. By the late 1990s, about 65 million American households subscribed to cable TV, with signals transmitted by wire from a central cable system. Many other watchers—including people living in remote locations—were able to receive television signals by setting up a satellite dish to receive signals from a telecommunications satellite. Some 137 satellite networks thrive today. They carry an enormous variety of programming. These systems

Many people use satellite dishes to receive television signals from communications satellites—especially in remote areas such as this neighborhood in Alaska.

spawned the first all-news network, CNN (Cable News Network), founded in 1980 and entirely devoted to various types of news programming. The network regularly runs programming on international news, business and sports, health, and entertainment. More than two hundred countries receive CNN news coverage through a related network, CNN International. CNN's ability to focus extensive resources on a big story first caught attention when its coverage became watched worldwide during the Persian Gulf War in 1991.

Others have followed, including MSNBC and Fox News Channel. However, CNN's own offspring, *Headline News*, is the only one that focuses just on straight news stories. *Headline News* thinks of itself as a "one-stop shopping center" for all the news, including weather, business, sports, finance, politics, entertainment, and events. Stories repeat, expand, or refresh every half hour. Its screen throws headlines, a team of anchors busily at work, and colorful slogans at the viewer all at once. With the focus on headlines, this kind of programming is the exact opposite of another programming innovation: the newsmagazine.

Newsmagazines

The introduction of newsmagazines marked a shift in programming that began some thirty-five years ago and completely transformed the face of news reporting. Newsmagazines changed the news from purely a public service to an integrated part of an entertainment industry, one that could make money.

The idea of selling television airtime is not new. Program sponsors have been buying television time for more than sixty years—ever since the early 1950s. (That is when TV viewing first became popular in the United States.) However, in the early days, stations and networks thought of news programs as a public service. They did not really expect these programs to make money. News programs were matter-of-fact and a little bit boring to many watchers. People watched the news to find out who won an election or how the nation's economy was doing. They did not expect to be amused or be entertained.

Then a news program called *60 Minutes* began to air in 1968.[1] Within a couple of years it had become enormously popular. This program was different. It told stories—not just isolated facts. It was less like a newspaper and more like a magazine. The stories were highly interesting, even sensational. They had a beginning, a middle, and a conclusion. Audiences found them absorbing and entertaining. They often learned about safety or tragedy or the lives of other people. *60 Minutes* attracted a lot of viewers, and made millions of dollars for its network.

In his book *Breaking the News*, journalist James Fallows comments, "*60 Minutes* changed TV journalism for one simple reason: it made money. Before the program's rise to popularity in the early 1970s, network news operations had been 'loss leaders.'"[2]

The Ratings Game

Remember the story of Christine Craft? Television ratings are powerful messages to television station and network executives. Ratings are the report cards that programming executives use to evaluate their decisions. The most famous and long-standing rating research firm is Nielsen Media Research, which has been measuring national and local television audiences for more than forty-five years. The company prides itself on its accuracy and independence. Each ratings point on a Nielsen rating represents over a million households—1,008,000, to be exact. So, if a program receives a rating of 4.9, that means people in 4.94 million homes were tuned in to that program on the night the ratings were taken. Does that sound like a lot? That is nothing. One blockbuster, NBC's *Friends*, received 20.0 points (20,160,000 homes) and another, *Frasier*, received 22.1 (22,276,800 homes) on one evening in May 2000. Does this mean these are really great shows? According to one critic, "Monster ratings are [a] sign of widespread popularity and not much else."[3] However, that popularity is what matters to the people who plan programming—and it matters a lot.

Nielsen uses a method known as statistical sampling. It is the same method used by polls to predict who will be elected president or governor or senator before all the ballots have been counted. Based on the percentage of the total possible audience in a region, the ratings wizards figure out how large a percentage of the national population was probably watching the program they are rating.

How do they know who is watching? They have several methods. Most of their information comes from meters that they have installed in about five thousand typical families' TV sets. The meters track what these families watch and when. The sampling of five thousand TV sets is not large, considering that about 99 million households have TV sets in the United States. However, Nielsen makes a big effort to make sure they find locations for their meters that represent the total picture as accurately as possible. Each household member logs in and out on a small black box near the TV set, so the ratings can reflect individuals as well as households.

To double-check the results, the company runs audits, quality checks, and comparisons. They also do random telephone interviews throughout the country to provide further information about who is watching what.

The published ratings determine the advertising rates for each program—so the higher the ratings, the higher the charge for a commercial time slot when it is airing. It would cost a lot more to be a sponsor of *Frasier*, for example, than for *Felicity* on the Warner Brothers Network (WB), with a rating of 2.0 (only 2,016,000 households). The ratings are powerful because millions of dollars are at stake.

The effect on the content and approach of television news has been as telling as anywhere else. Television news veteran Walter Cronkite expressed his concern about television newsmagazines in a quote that appeared in the *Columbia Journalism Review* in 1998: "Instead of offering tough documentaries and background on the issues that so deeply affect all of us," he noted, "they're turning those programs into television copies of *Photoplay* magazine." The situation made many hardworking television newspeople unhappy. "But," said Cronkite, "they are helpless when top management demands an increase in ratings to protect profits."[4]

1 HUT	$\dfrac{6}{10}$	$\dfrac{\text{Households Using TV}}{\text{Total TV Households}}$	=	**60%**
2 Rating	$\dfrac{3}{10}$	$\dfrac{\text{Channel 2 Households}}{\text{Total TV Households}}$	=	**30%**
3 Share	$\dfrac{3}{6}$	$\dfrac{\text{Channel 2 Households}}{\text{Households Using TV}}$	=	**50%**

or Rating = Share x HUT

HUT stands for "households using TV" on a given day. In this illustration, only six out of ten are using TV. Of those six households, three (50%) are watching Channel 2. These ratings hold high importance for the amount a station or network can charge for advertising.

In his book *Broadcasting Realities*, Ken Lindner writes:

> Years ago when television news was in its infancy, news divisions were non-profit making entities. Their lofty goal was to serve the public interest. They viewed their responsibility as that of a public trust. . . . But, when it was discovered that huge sums of money could be made in news . . . TV journalism became a competition for viewers, demographics and ratings.[5]

Lindner says that one local news manager once told him he broke down the ratings of his local newscasts into three-minute segments. This method allowed him to compare his news ratings from day to day. He could find out exactly which stories attracted viewers and which ones caused viewers to turn his program off. "With this information," Lindner says, "he then decides which stories to continue to run in a later newscast, or the next day."[6]

Sponsor Power

Sponsors play a vital and powerful role in commercial television programming decisions. Their influence on news programs raises real cause for concern.

As news anchor Dan Rather puts it,

> They've got us putting more and more fuzz and wuzz on the air, cop-shop stuff, so as to compete not with other news programs but with entertainment programs (including those posing as news programs) for dead bodies, mayhem, and lurid tales. . . . It is fear of ratings slippage, if not failure, fear that this

quarter's bottom line will not be better than last quarter's—and a whole lot better than the same quarter's a year ago. A climate of fear, at all levels, has been created.[7]

The system tends to skew the coverage toward those who have the money to buy the sponsor's products. As Neil Postman and Steve Powers observe in their book, *How To Watch TV News*, news shows generally appeal to a more affluent, better educated, and more attentive portion of the television audience. So, they are "a prime target for advertisers trying to reach an affluent market." As a result, "sponsors are willing to pour money into well-produced commercials," Postman and Powers point out. "These spots are often longer in length than most news stories and certainly cost more to produce than what's going into the content of the news."[8] In return, of course, these sponsors demand that the television news shows attract the viewers who will respond to their commercials. That, in fact, television news shows— like every other aspect of television—become winners in the ratings game that dominates every decision made about a television show's content. Whether situation comedy, reality-based shows such as *Survivor*, made-for-television movies, or news broadcasts, the job of each show is quite simply to produce viewers of commercials.

So Much News, So Little Time

Television news is geared for people on the move, not for people who like to read and analyze. Its purpose is to deliver news in an entertaining way that will attract viewers.

Anchor Ted Koppel offers sharp criticism of this limited view of TV news, however. He writes,

> Those with the inclination can find everything they want and need in print, on NPR [National Public Radio] or on the Internet. But the networks, which still reach the largest audiences, are cutting back on stories they might once have felt an obligation to cover— especially foreign news. The most accessible media are devolving into the least useful and daring. The educationally and economically deprived in our society, who used to receive at least some exposure to information they might not have selected for themselves, but from which they might have received some benefit, are now reduced to watching only what we believe they want; and we have little confidence in their appetite or range.[9]

The journalist's job is always haunted by deadlines. As Neil Postman and Steve Powers point out, the pressure of time presents a constant obstacle for TV journalists. "Time works against understanding, coherence, and even meaning," Postman and Powers write. "The practical needs of a show, especially getting on the air at a specific time, call for the reporter to do the best he can under the circumstances."[10]

Time constraints scarcely leave journalists time to pin down the verifiable truth. On-the-spot, real-time coverage provides immediacy and excitement but not the long view. Since TV news, like all television, must compete in the game for ratings and profits, it has to appeal to viewer tastes, at the expense of a more demanding presentation. In the face of all these and other hurdles, many news researchers, writers, anchors, and the rest of the television news team work hard to gather and report the news honestly. But it is not an easy job, and the system often works against them.

Keeping the Audience Tuned In

Even for public broadcasting, the challenge is always to get the audience to tune in and then to keep their attention. Robert MacNeil, former co-anchor of the PBS news show *The MacNeil-Lehrer Report*, explained the philosophy behind much of television newscasting when he said that the idea is to "keep everything brief, not to strain the attention of anyone but instead to provide constant stimulation through variety, novelty, action, and movement. . . . bite-sized is best . . . complexity must be avoided. . . ."[11] One of the most respected news shows on public television, the MacNeil-Lehrer Report broke most of these "rules" and attempted to offer longer and more-in-depth stories. The program had a huge success among many thoughtful television viewers, but the show never came close to capturing a fraction of the audience that watched the more formula-bound, faster-paced commercial television news programs.

Among the commercial news programs there can be a roar of competition. Trivial information may be trumpeted as if it were important—especially if it is flashy and immediate. Frequently, TV news programs (as well as newspapers) pay little attention to issues that develop more quietly and take longer to consider, absorb, and understand—even though they may be more important in the long run. Journalists are not really to blame. The public clamors to be entertained and ignores what is not exciting.

The media has responded as anyone might expect. A survey done by the Rocky Mountain Media Watch showed some interesting results, published in the July 1997 issue of the *Columbia Journalism Review (CJR)*. The Media Watch tracked the contents of one hundred local newscasts around the nation to get a feel for what kinds of stories the stations felt were most important. The results were taken on the last day of the February sweeps—a key ratings event, when TV programming planners try to run their most alluring programs to get the highest ratings possible. The results showed that fifty-nine of the lead stories dealt with crime. Another thirteen focused on disasters. About 43 percent of all news airtime (aside from sports and weather), *CJR* reported, was devoted to crime, disaster, war, or terrorism. By contrast, less than 2.5 percent of the total news time covered less sensational issues such as education, arts, science, children, poverty, and civil rights. *CJR* pointed out that these slighted topics were "the kind of things that mean more to a community's long term health than one night's killing or one day's mudslide."[12]

Reuven Frank, a former president of NBC News, decries the "give them what they want" attitude he sees in the broadcasting industry. He calls the argument that

*Many news stations use the rule of thumb, "If it bleeds, it leads."
So, often the first story to air on a news program may focus on a
bloody accident, a tragic story, or heavy storm damage.*

journalists have to provide what people want a "dope
pusher's argument." He says that news, by definition,
is not interesting to people until they hear about it, so
how can they know what they want? "The job of a journalist," he asserts, "is to take what's important and
make it interesting."[13]

Frank may be stretching his point a little bit. If
we have heard that there was a big earthquake in San
Francisco, of course we want to hear about it and we
have a right to know more details. But, he rightly
points out, there are many things that happen in the

world that are of importance to us that we are not aware of. These events are also news and may have even greater significance to us in the long run than the San Francisco earthquake.

News vs. Entertainment

So, in the interest of attracting viewers, producers use colorful graphics, tightly edited sound bites, and joking newscast personalities to turn news events into fast-paced, bright entertainment. Little can be explored with much depth or thoughtfulness, and the subject matter tends to be emotional, alarming, or light.

"Having trouble losing weight? More and more people are turning to liposuction!" might be the opening tease for one night's local newscast. "Stock analysts turn to psychics to help them predict business trends," might announce another newscast. So-called "life-style" news has become a regular item on most television news broadcasts. When television news is not covering sensational news, it often turns to trendy topics. During a flurry of "reality" entertainment shows such as *Survivor* in 2000–2001, some network television news shows spent more and more time promoting their network's reality entertainment shows. Writing for the *Columbia Journalism Review*, Lawrence K. Grossman, former president of both NBC News and PBS, observes that some news programs seem willing to "shill for the network's prime time 'reality' entertainment shows in the vain hope that their popularity will rub off on its [own] offerings."[14] One newsmagazine devoted an entire hour to the *Survivor* craze. In fact, in August 2000, TV newsmagazines devoted ninety-seven segments to *Survivor*.

Are News Programs Objective?

The truth is, human beings are not objective. However, readers and viewers need to be able to trust the news. For trust to become possible, two things have to happen: Journalists must strive to become aware of their own biases, always make their sources clear, and recognize the limitations of their own knowledge. At the same time, viewers and readers need to know how to recognize bias when they hear and see it—and they need to make mental adjustments for it. A good rule of thumb is to recognize that few things are as certain as proponents try to make them seem. Here are a few ways bias creeps into the news.[15]

(1) **Only partly true.** Editors, producers, and writers shape the news we see by selecting what they think is important or interesting. Obviously, they do not have time to tell all the details or even to cover all the news. With this selection and omission process, bias automatically occurs. Some details may be ignored—intentionally or unintentionally— and viewers may therefore form a different opinion than they otherwise would. What is the best way for a viewer to offset this effect? Compare news reports from a wide variety of sources—including radio, newspaper, magazines, different TV networks, and the

Internet. Time does not often permit exploring all these avenues, but the more points of view one samples, the broader the view of what is really happening.

Sometimes, though, news programs may leave viewers frustrated by the questions that they do not answer—and may not even try to answer. In May 2002, writer Rob Walker watched the evening news programs of each of the three major news networks, ABC, CBS, and NBC. He concluded overall that more questions get answered on talk shows than on national network news programs. On ABC's *World News Tonight* with Peter Jennings, one segment's introduction began: "The Senate Judiciary Committee today agreed to delay the vote on a controversial White House nomination to a federal court." This seemed about to introduce some meaty discussion of the controversy. But no. Footage showed two senators, Orrin Hatch and Patrick Leahy, bickering in a side debate. Peter Jennings asked the audience whether the two senators were aware that they might be heard—since apparently their microphones were on. After "eavesdropping" for about a minute, Jennings asked his question again: "Did they or did they not know their microphones were open?" That was all. But this was only a small fraction of the story. Jennings did not mention who the person nominated was. He did not mention even what court the nomination was for. The video clip and its argument did not give any clues, Walker says.[16]

What was the purpose of this clip? To inform? To discredit the two senators in some way? How could even a well-informed viewer get more than innuendo out of a clip such as this one? It certainly gave only the most superficial glimpse of what was going on— when one of the great advantages of TV news is the ability to show what is happening. At best, this coverage gave only a partial glimpse of the truth.

(2) **The power of the lead story.** The news director and producers of a news program choose the lead story and the sequence of all other news items in the program. These choices produce bias through placement. The story's position placement in the program also signals a sense of its importance. Newspaper articles that are out of view in the back pages seem less significant than those featured on the front page. The same principle works for a television news show. Television broadcasts run stories that draw ratings first—giving them apparent importance. Especially because of this special motive, the lead story may not really be the most important.

(3) **It's all in the camera angle.** Photography can be used to introduce bias. A sweep of a camera around a cluttered office may distract from the ideas a subject is expressing. A

camera angle may make someone look unpleasant. The photos and film clips an editor chooses can have a big influence on the audience's opinions.

(4) **Loaded words and names.** Words carried in captions or spoken by an anchor or reporter also can convey bias. Positive or negative words can be loaded with emotions—and those emotions can have a strong influence on the viewer. Words used to characterize a person's actions, such as "freedom fighter" or "terrorist," carry considerable clout and influence listeners. Even a tone of voice or inflection may introduce a negative or positive note.

(5) **Bias from the "experts."** Many news programs bring in experts to comment on issues. However, how expert are they? Are their credentials clear, and how unbiased are they? What is their background? Are opposing viewpoints also given? Why do the same "experts" show up so often?

4

When Trust Is in Danger

When do viewers begin to question the trustworthiness of what they see? Better yet, When *should* they question it? A few key signals can alert watchful viewers that other motives are beginning to come into play. Sensationalism is probably one of the biggest and easiest to spot. Sensationalist news coverage centers on lurid crimes and graphic displays of bloody scenes. It does not take time to put crimes into the context of patterns or trends. It does not offer a discussion of issues. It plays on fear and emotion and distrust of different lifestyles and cultures. Sensationalist news is opportunistic—that is, it takes advantage of emotional scenes and stories to make money. It is a tradition known as "yellow journalism"—the practice of distorting or exploiting to create excitement, also known as sensationalism, or *tabloid* news.

Sensationalism in News Coverage

Tabloid news is not unique to television. In fact, it has been around for a long time. It is the kind of news found in those sensational magazines and "newspapers" found next to the checkout counters in the local supermarket. Some, such as the *National Enquirer*, focus on celebrities, and have such headlines as "Bad-Girl Britney Goes Dirty Dancing," and "Judge Judy Cheats on Husband."[1] Even less reputable tabloids, such as the *Weekly World News*, contain stories that show little concern for accuracy or even believability. They have headlines such as "Bat Boy Found in W. Virginia Cave"[2] and "Aliens Capture Top-Secret NASA Moon Base."[3] These stories sell papers but make no pretense of telling the truth. And most people understand that—so few people are fooled.

Tabloid news has a long, if not always honorable, tradition—it began a century ago, in 1901. The idea of publishing sensational news existed even before that time, but the tabloid newspaper was about 11 by 15 inches and was easy to hold. It used a lot of illustrations. These lively newspapers presented the news in short, upbeat, amusing articles. They also focused on crime and sex and disaster.

Tiny UFO Lands in Man's Garden:
Mini Crop Circles Mark Landing Site

Bigfoot Trapped in Telephone Booth

Dog Gives Birth to Ducklings:
Idaho Farmer Amazed

Weird Disease Turns People into Stone

Man Falls 3,000 Feet Without Parachute
—And Lives!

110-YEAR-OLD BRAZILIAN WOMAN SKATEBOARDS 10 MILES A DAY TO KEEP IN SHAPE

Giant Dinosaur Discovered Alive in Amazon: *Swedish Explorers Amazed*

Woman Goes Back in Time—Saves Own Grandmother:
"If I hadn't done it I wouldn't be here today!"

Tabloid headlines astound readers.

What Is a News Story?

Other distortions of straight news may be more difficult to identify. Since news has become entertainment, viewers expect to be drawn into a news item. Producers and news teams think of themselves as charged with the job of making the news interesting and absorbing. Part of this is a legacy from the newsmagazines, and it is not necessarily bad—but it does place a twist on the news that audiences view.

Many of the news stories that appear on *60 Minutes* and other newsmagazine shows are really constructed as carefully as short stories. Unlike most straight news stories, they have a beginning, a middle, and an end. Many feature a news reporter in the role of crusading newsperson or persistent detective. Often, too, they are out to investigate a bad guy, often associated with a large corporation or some other powerful authority. Or they seek to right a wrong. The world of newsmagazines is a world in which the average man or woman is seen in constant battle with forces much larger than himself or herself. As in mystery books, we usually follow the news reporter, our hero Mike, Dan, or Morley, as he leads us through the narrative and takes us safely to the satisfying conclusion of the tale.

Normally, of course, real news events are seldom so neat and rarely offer such a clearly defined narrative path. But it is important to remember that the stories that these newsmagazines choose to present to their viewers are only the stories that can be shaped to fit the requirements of the narrative. And, while the usual amount of time spent on a news event in a national or local news show may be a minute or two long, the newsmagazines may give up to fifteen or twenty minutes to their feature stories.

Television newsmagazines are called "magazines" because they are more like magazines than they are like newspapers. They run fewer stories and do not try to cover the daily news events of the day. They do not attempt to present the breaking news events of the day, but instead offer "feature stories"—that is, stories that they think will both inform and entertain their viewers but are not necessarily related to the day's news events. So, they can afford to spend more time on each story. They can begin preparing their stories weeks and sometimes even months before the stories are aired. That is a luxury that the daily television news shows do not usually have. Although sometimes short feature stories are run during a straight daily news show, these are generally much shorter and much more quickly put together than the feature stories on the magazine shows.

Who Is Checking the Facts?

Occasionally, television news producers are so eager for an interesting or amusing human-interest story that they grab it and put it on the air without checking far enough into its truth or validity. It is "light stuff" anyway, the reasoning goes, and no one will remember it the day after tomorrow.

Just such an incident occurred in 1959, during television's still-youthful days. But in this case the story did not go away—it caught on and was picked up by other television news shows, radio broadcasts, and even newspapers and magazines. In fact, the story kept being put before the public months after its original television broadcast. It was a good, funny story, it had eccentric people and animals—two surefire audience pleasers—and it was easy to understand. Unfortunately it was also a hoax. It did not start out that way. It actually started out as a practical joke by a clever writer who wanted to protest extremist thinking and censorship. The problem was that it was just too funny a story for the media to let go, especially on slow news days, or when television producers needed something light and amusing to balance up their newscast. By the time the truth came out, the story, and other follow-up stories, had run for over six years.

It all began when a professional writer and publicist named Alan Abel rented a door to a broom closet in a respectable building in New York City. Abel did not need the broom closet. He just wanted the door so that he could affix a handsome-looking sign to it. The sign read:

SINA NATIONAL HEADQUARTERS
G. CLIFFORD PROUT JR., PRESIDENT
ALAN ABEL, VICE-PRESIDENT

The broom closet was always kept locked. It worked out better that way. SINA also was given a listed telephone number, MO–rality 1–1963. But what was SINA? Well, the acronym stood for the Society for Indecency to Naked Animals. And, according to press statements issued by G. Clifford Prout Jr., the president, it was organized to combat the incredible public indecency of hundreds of thousands of naked animals running around. What SINA was campaigning for, according to Prout, was putting clothes, or at least pants or diapers, on all these embarrassed and embarrassing creatures. That meant, according to Prout, everything from elephants and horses to dogs and cats, ducks and canaries. Now, Prout sounded like a pretty strange creature himself, but of course there really was no G. Clifford Prout. Like the SINA office headquarters, he was completely imaginary. But when newspapers and television network producers began to respond to the press releases and contact SINA's vice president, Abel decided he needed to produce the president. An actor-writer friend of his named Buck Henry was recruited for the part. Soon, to Abel's delight and mystification, both he and G. Clifford Prout began to appear to promote their cause on many network television news shows such as Walter Cronkite's *CBS News* and NBC's *The Today Show*.

Abel was certain that the media would catch on to his joke, but he hoped that maybe a few would go along with it. He was stunned to find that many media people were taking it seriously. Everyone was taking it so seriously, in fact, that within a year, a number of local communities had formed SINA groups of their own and were actually putting clothes on their pets. At one point, protesters even picketed the White House, demanding that Jacqueline Kennedy, the president's wife, put pants on her favorite riding horse.

Had the media caught on to the joke and decided to go along with it? Or had their thirst for human-interest news stories overridden their critical faculties, keeping them from seeing through the hoax? It was probably a little bit of both. One thing was certain, though: While many people may have played along with the joke, a lot of people took the

SINA guidelines suggested dressing animals in clothing, so they might look something like this.

whole thing seriously—so seriously that during the six years it continued, both Abel and his actor friend appeared on numerous television news and magazine shows promoting their "cause." Finally, in 1966, Abel published a book, *The Great American Hoax*, revealing the whole hilarious SINA story.

Another notorious television news hoax, the Tamara Rand affair, was not quite so funny or so innocent. This one originated in 1981 on a Las Vegas television talk show called *Dick Maurice and Company*, produced on station KNTV. Although the *Dick Maurice and Company* show was not a news show, the appearance on that show of a so-called psychic named Tamara Rand kicked off news stories that had television news shows around the country buzzing for days.

Rand had made an appearance on the Dick Maurice show in January 1981. Two months later, on March 30, 1981, a disturbed young man named John Hinckley, Jr., attempted to assassinate the president of the United States, Ronald Reagan, outside a Washington, D.C., hotel. The president was seriously wounded when a bullet entered his left side, stopping only a few inches from his heart, and three other people were also injured in the assassination attempt. Hinckley was instantly captured and arrested at the scene. Within hours, Tamara Rand called television news stations with an announcement that she had predicted the assassination attempt, complete with details, on her appearance on the *Dick Maurice and Company* television show two months earlier in

January. And, she said, she had a tape of that show to prove it.

Had Rand really predicted the attempted assassination months before it happened? The tape she produced appeared to prove it. On the tape, Rand certainly did predict that a fair-haired young man (Hinckley was light-haired) named "Jack Humley" (it appeared a pretty close fit) would attempt to kill the president and "fire shots all over the place." As fantastic as it sounded, the story appeared to be true and Rand and her "prediction" were quickly featured in local and network television news stories. Too quickly, as it turned out.

A few days after running the story on their news shows, the major networks were admitting that the story was untrue and the Rand tape and predictions were a fraud. A careful review of the tape revealed some disturbing facts. Rings on Rand's fingers appeared to change magically from one kind to another and from one shot to another, and the microphone used on the show also appeared to keep changing places abruptly. Also, disturbingly, while reviewing the station's copy of the January tape of the Dick Maurice show, the news director of KTNV, where it had originally aired, discovered that Rand had never made the prediction on the show.

Questioned, Maurice was forced to admit that the prediction and the tape were hoaxes. In March, *after* the assassination attempt on President Reagan, wearing the same clothes and using the same sets as in the original show, Rand and Maurice had taped the so-called "prediction" that supposedly had appeared on the January show. Then they had inserted the newly taped material into a copy of the original January tape. Maurice admitted that Rand was a good friend, and he wanted to help her in her career as a psychic. Many people today still talk about the amazing "predictions" of so-called psychics and use the Tamara Rand story as an example of the power of psychic ability.

The Lure of the Great Story

Sometimes newspeople, especially those doing investigative journalism, fall in love with their story. Like lovers who only see what they look for in their beloved, they may overlook facts or statements that may not agree with their estimation. They may interpret other facts or statements in a way that appears to confirm what they want to find or hear but in reality may not actually confirm their beliefs at all. Such apparently was the case with a team of CNN newspeople in 1998 when a CNN newsmagazine show broadcast the now infamous "Tailwind" report.

At the time, CNN was taking a beating in the ratings. Their twenty four-hour news format had been a revolutionary breakthrough in television news, but the network always drew its highest ratings when there was a big news story to feature. A major natural disaster, a political upheaval, a sensational murder case, a war—whenever these big events occurred, people turned to CNN for its extensive coverage. For the news-only network, the problem was that such big stories did not happen every day. On so-called "slow news days," the audience would tune in for a few minutes, catch what was happening, and then turn to the other networks to see what was on.

The solution, CNN decided, was to build a news-magazine show, similar to what the other networks were offering. Patterned after the broadcast networks' newsmagazine programs, it would feature an assortment of stories tailored to the viewer's interests, some human-interest bits, some "soft news," health-related features and celebrity profiles, and some "investigative reporting."

In the process, CNN ran a story that claimed that U.S. military personnel had used a toxic nerve agent called sarin against U.S. Army deserters in Laos during the Vietnam War. The story was picked up by *Time* magazine. The charges made were serious and, amid objections from the Pentagon and veterans of the war, CNN requested an investigation by an independent attorney. The attorney concluded that the story had no foundation in fact, and CNN had to retract the story.

Ted Koppel remarked:

> In the old days, we at least gave lip service to the notion that we would wait to report a story until we got most of the facts straight. The imperatives of 'live' television, however, are different. They demand a constant patter of commentary and conversation on the story of the moment, even when nothing but the most basic information (for example, there's been an outbreak of shooting inside the Armenian parliament) is known.[4]

The pressure of competition is so intense that news programs are compelled to keep up with each other. A newscaster is reluctant to admit that not all the information is available for fear of losing viewers to another program—one that possibly is not checking facts so carefully but seems to have the whole story now, not later. "We of the television news industry," Koppel says, "have no greater fear than that of a viewer's finger on the remote control."[5]

The Interview

Interviews are generally a lot less straightforward than most people think. It is important to realize that the taped or filmed interview that viewers see on a television news program does not necessarily represent the actual interview as it happened in real time. On a network news show like *60 Minutes*, for instance, the actual interview may have taken over an hour's worth of tape, while the portion that you see may only run for five minutes of airtime. This means that the television viewer never sees about fifty five minutes of the real-life interview. What has been left out? How many clarifying or qualifying statements have been lost?

During the interview, did the astronomer say, "Yes, some astronomers believe in flying saucers. But the vast majority of them do not"—only to see himself later on TV, in a cut and edited tape, flatly remarking, "Yes, some astronomers believe in flying saucers"? No hint remains of his disclaimer. He had intended only to be agreeable and then clarify—but the clarification got lost on the cutting-room floor.

Or, imagine a politician being asked to comment on the news from the previous day that the small country of Freedonia might be selling yo-yos to U.S. citizens at prices much lower than manufacturers in the United States, thus endangering America's yo-yo industries. Perhaps during the entire interview as it was originally taped, the politician was unsure of himself, stumbled around a lot in his answers, and was something less than knowledgeable:

"Well, Bob, I really don't know too much about that yet. . . . It's a breaking issue, um, I have done some preliminary thinking about it, though, and my guess would be that, well, probably we should hold back a little, you know, maybe temporarily ban trade with them until we have a fuller view of the situation and then, you know, make our decisions accordingly." After the tape has been edited, though, the senator's comments may sound much more direct and dynamic, however misleading.

Interviewer Bob: "Tell me, Senator, what do you think we should do about the Freedonia situation?"

Politician: "Ban trade with them."

A couple of seconds of expensive broadcast time have been saved, but an accurate account of what the politician actually said and how he said it has been lost.

Reverse Questions

Many television news shows also employ the "reverse-question" technique. That is, an interview is conducted by a reporter with a camera pointed solely at the person being interviewed. Later, another filming takes place with a camera then pointed at the reporter who is seen asking the questions to which the interviewed person earlier replied. The technique was used originally by small stations that only had one camera to work with. But its advantages soon became obvious, as Peter Funt explains in Richard Campbell's book *60 Minutes and The News: A Mythology for Middle America*:

> Although the networks insist that reverse questions match the original questions as closely as possible, there is no denying that the reporter is allowed to polish his performance while the interview subject's answers must stand as first delivered.[6]

Interviewer Barbara Walters adds,

> One of the advantages for the reporter is that he always comes out on top; he's always right. You've never seen a *60 Minutes* interview, or any taped interview, in which the reporter gets the worst of it.[7]

Another advantage, of course, is that the reporter, having already seen the response to his questions, may, during the later filming, add little dramatic gestures or intonations to his questions that then may subtly alter the viewer's perception of the tone of the story or the answers given by his subject. A wonderful example of this can be seen in the 1987 fictitious movie *Broadcast News*. Here, as the story is being put together for broadcast, the television news reporter watches the tape as a woman he has interviewed earlier in the day answers one of his questions with a sad and tragic story. The reporter repeats for the camera the question he asked earlier. This time, though, before he asks his next question he stops his cameraman for a moment and makes him wait as he forces tears to slowly come into his eyes to help dramatize his human side—showing an unreal sympathy for the woman and her answer to his previous question.

Photo Opportunities

A picture is always selective—the image chosen, the way it is framed, the way it is lit, and everything in it. Politicians learned a lesson about the power of the television image during the first presidential debate between Richard Nixon and John F. Kennedy. While Kennedy appeared relaxed and self-assured, Nixon's perspiring face and visible whisker growth made him look less trustworthy and confident. That image helped Kennedy defeat Nixon in the 1960 election.

Years later, Newt Gingrich, Speaker of the U.S. House of Representatives, also used a television image to create an impression. While standing in front of CSPAN cameras, Gingrich would make impassioned speeches, complete with gestures and knowing looks at his unseen audience. But the audience was unseen because it was not there. The House chambers were often completely empty during these speeches—but Gingrich played to the empty seats anyway. He knew that with the CSPAN camera locked into position only on the speaker's podium, the television viewers would believe that he was making an important speech before a full house. His dramatic gesturing and feigned eye contact with a nonexistent audience might have looked a little bit silly to any other house member who looked in the door, but Gingrich knew that what the television viewers thought was happening was more important than the reality.[8]

During the 1992 presidential campaign, a television news crew taking pictures of Vice President Dan Quayle showed him waving at empty fields, with no human beings in sight, from the back platform of his campaign train. A short time later, as the train pulled into another stop, the same crew shot pictures of a large crowd waving at the campaign train. The news crew that had actually taken the pictures was later upset to find that when their video footage hit the airwaves the two separate events had been edited together, making it appear to be only one event, showing the vice president greeting and being greeted by an admiring throng.

In these days of super-fast computers and high technology, remember too that television images can also be deliberately faked. An advertisement that ran during the 2001 Super Bowl showed actor Christopher Reeve, who had been paralyzed in a horse-riding accident in 1995, rising to his feet and walking. The actor, best known for his appearances as Superman in the movies, was shown to be standing among a gathering in an auditorium that was supposed to be a future event in which awards would be given for research into spinal cord injuries. An investment company promoting investments in the industry presented the advertisement. While the faked footage of Reeve, who is completely paralyzed from the neck

When Vice President Richard Nixon appeared on a televised presidential debate, viewers found him nervous and unattractive in comparison with the more charismatic John Kennedy. That image helped Kennedy win the 1960 election. Here Nixon wipes perspiration off his face.

down, was defended by the advertisers, others argued that it gave false hope to people with similar injuries.

During the coverage of New Year's Eve celebrations as the clock ticked down to 2001, Dan Rather and the CBS news crew offered viewers an attractive, busy view out the window looking down into Times Square. What viewers did not know, though, was that one of the large billboards that they could see very vividly in the square was not there at all. Using digital technology, CBS inserted a fake billboard—an advertisement for themselves—over two real billboards. The throngs of people crowded in the square that night could easily see the two real billboards. But the television audiences saw something completely different. While the television audience believed that the live television coverage was showing them reality, it was actually showing them an altered and faked fictional view.

A more serious example—a faked news story—occurred in 1993 when NBC news presented a sensational story on its *Dateline NBC* newsmagazine show. The feature story, called "Waiting to Explode," claimed to be an exposé of the dangerous design of pickup trucks manufactured by General Motors (GM) between 1973 and 1987. The truck's gas tanks, claimed NBC, could rupture easily and explode if the truck was hit broadside in a traffic accident, even at low speeds. Television viewers watching that night saw a dramatic video of a Chevrolet truck exploding into flames when it was struck by a relatively slow-moving passenger vehicle. The test crash, NBC asserted, was forceful evidence of their claims about the GM truck's shocking vulnerability. The only problem was that prior to the show, NBC's attempts to ignite the truck's gas tanks in their test collisions had all failed miserably. The tanks simply would not explode at the speed and conditions that NBC had claimed. In order to provide the television audience with explosive visual proof of their claims against

GM, NBC rigged the tests. They equipped the test truck with hidden explosives, which they ignited by radio control at the moment of the impact. The devastating fire that viewers watched was actually caused by the ignition of the explosives and not by the impact of the passenger car. NBC's fakery was exposed when GM ran tests of their own, after NBC had refused to allow the automobile manufacturer to inspect the damaged remains of the two vehicles. NBC was forced to offer a humiliating on-the-air apology for their faked news story.

Two years later, another major incident occurred when CBS corporate executives caved in to pressure from a big tobacco company, Brown & Williamson (makers of Kool, Pall Mall Filtered, Viceroy, and many other cigarette brands). Mike Wallace of *60 Minutes* had prepared a taped interview with Jeffrey Wigand, former vice president of research at B&W. Wigand had evidence that cigarette manufacturers deliberately raised nicotine levels to increase addiction in smokers. He also showed that cigarette manufacturers had deliberately lied to Congress in their testimony under oath about addiction to nicotine. CBS knew the information in the interview was accurate and important for the public to know. Yet, CBS executives feared B&W would sue, and even if CBS won, the defense could run as high as ten or fifteen billion dollars. Such a suit could possibly bankrupt the corporation. So they did not run the segment. A 1999 movie, *The Insider*, told the tale, though not completely accurately.

A Tough Dilemma

Television news, of course, is not alone in sometimes misleading or misinforming the public. It does not deserve to bear all the guilt in a world where everyone may move a little bit too fast to allow for accuracy and many media may blur the boundaries between truth and fiction. That, however, is only a sad and broader commentary on the dilemmas of our time. Also, television has a heavy responsibility. In today's world, television is the primary source of news for most people. Newspapers still have readers and radios still have listeners, but neither competes with the millions of people who get their news from television each day.

The choices, everyone agrees, are tough ones. "All of us in commercial television are confronted by a difficult choice that commercialism imposes," Ted Koppel admits. But does that burden excuse laxity? He asks:

> Do we deliberately aim for the lowest common denominator, thereby assuring ourselves of the largest possible audience but producing nothing but cotton candy for the mind, or do we tackle difficult subjects as creatively as we can, knowing that we may lose much of the mass audience?[9]

5

Some Tricks of the Trade

To draw in people and keep them tuned in, news programs make use of a special bag of tricks. They try to create an entertaining tone. Whether on a national network or local station, the goal is always the same: Hold the viewers' attention. Do not let those hands wander to the channel changer. Losing the interest of the audience may cause cancellation of a sponsor's support and certainly will mean lost money.

Building a Winning News Team

Local news stations like to build an anchor team of personalities that work well together. The members of the team are warm and personable. They are attractive. They get along with each other. They joke and banter, like members of a family. By creating the homey feel of a family atmosphere, station executives hope to build bonds between the audience and the program's stars. So, the lead male anchor may often be fatherly and gently authoritative. The lead female anchor must be pretty and well groomed. (This unspoken rule has been challenged by former Kansas City news anchor Christine Craft.[1])

"Well, Connie," the anchor may ask the weatherperson, "What kind of a day are you going to give us tomorrow?" (As if the weather person had some kind of control over the weather.) "Jerry, it is going to be a beautiful day!" the weathercaster smiles proudly.

Then it is the sportscaster's turn. "Well, John, what is going on with those Yankees?" the other anchorperson may ask. "They're just going crazy these days, Mary!" the sports announcer replies enthusiastically. The anchors exchange good-natured jokes with the sports announcer before he launches into the sports news. The mood is usually light and airy. Banter among the sportscaster, weather reporter, and anchors tends to be upbeat.

Much of the news is serious, dramatic, frightening, or tragic. These stories are delivered with appropriately somber attitudes. However, the friendly, seemingly spontaneous banter that occurs interspersed between the "serious" business of the news reaffirms the friendly family atmosphere. The ratings show that

Students in college learn to imitate the "winning formula" for television news. Here students shoot a news program for HC-TV, produced and managed by Huntington College in Indiana.

this formula works, and few local stations venture far away from it.

Network news programs have a national or even a worldwide audience. So, they build a different kind of atmosphere—usually more dramatic and sophisticated. Depending on the news, the anchors may act somber or upbeat. Usually, though, they show flair, stage presence (the ability to look smooth and unflustered), and personality.

Traditionally, in journalism, reporters not only reported the news, they also gathered the news. As pressures changed and roles evolved in television news, that tradition began to change—at least for TV news. Anchors now rarely gather the news.

Even today, though, many watchers assume that the people they see on the screen are also involved in gathering the news. In the early days of TV, that may have been true. Television newsmagazines changed that, though. For a newsmagazine's story, people behind the scenes often work for months. These producers and researchers find the facts, film the segments, and even write the scripts for the "reporters" people see on screen.

Journalist James Fallows describes the preparation in his book *Breaking the News*:

> They follow up leads from the newspapers, they collect tips, they camp in small towns for two weeks to line up the right sources for the filmed interviews. When everything is in place, but not until then, the stars are brought in to ask questions with the camera turned on.[2]

The anchors—or on a newsmagazine, the interviewers—are the stars of the show. However, as far as putting the story together is concerned, they are just "window dressing"—showpieces like the displays in store windows, designed to attract interest. They are the "talent," in TV jargon. In reality, they are just readers, or messengers. Their job is to deliver the news to the audience. Someone else developed the ideas and did most of the work.

A newsmagazine is produced much like any other television show. So, some journalists who value the old tradition feel that their profession has become cheapened. As Fallows puts it, the idea became accepted

> that you could be a celebrated broadcast "journalist" while neglecting the most vital functions of the 'traditional' reporter. . . . To the viewer it looks as if Diane or Ed or Mike has been on the story from the start, since we see them in the basic journalistic act of interviewing. But these "journalists" have usually arrived only a day or two earlier, and they will fly out as soon as the shooting is done so they can jump into another story someplace else.[3]

To get an idea how many people work behind the scenes to gather up the facts of a television news story, take a look at the long list of credits that runs at the end of the program.

What difference does all this make? Only this: As viewers, we cannot take what we see at face value—because the face we see is not fully responsible for what we hear and see. The people who are responsible are mostly offscreen. We are watching a carefully prepared show.

Does that necessarily mean we cannot trust the news? No. It only means that we need to be aware of the layers of responsibility. We need to understand that some degree of accountability may be lost. We also need to understand the tremendous pressures of time, logistics, and priorities under which every news program operates. Most news programs strive to provide accurate news. However, the process is complex and difficult—and sometimes they make mistakes.

Weather reporters work with complex maps to show weather conditions and forecasts.

The Awards Game

How many awards for TV news can there be? Surely there must be many more than most of us can imagine, since just about every television station from the largest in New York and Los Angeles, to the smallest in Ohio, Arizona, and Wyoming, likes to announce at the opening of their news shows, "And now, Channel X's award-winning news team!" What are these awards, who gives them out, and what are they for? Many viewers might imagine the award was for the news team's keen analysis. But for all the viewers know, the Cleveland Hairdresser's Association may have given an award to the station's anchorperson, or maybe the weatherman, for the best hairstyle on local television news. So maybe the real award winner was the backstage hairstylist.

This misinterpretation may be as much the fault of the viewers as of the news producer or the station manager. Many legitimate awards are made for values in news production that have nothing to do with the quality of the news reporting. For example, the Academy of Television Arts and Sciences bestows Emmy awards each year for such categories as "Outstanding Coverage of a News Story—Programs" and "Outstanding Investigative Journalism—Programs." Yet Emmy awards are also granted for outstanding achievement by an art director or scenic designer. Other Emmy categories include sound editing, sound mixing, special visual effects, and so on. These categories have value, but they do not convey the same message about the quality of the program's content that "Outstanding Coverage of a News Story" does.

So, it makes sense to be skeptical about the claim that a program is "award-winning." Look at it this way: If the award is for strong news content, the station will probably say so. Otherwise, it may be fair to assume, at the very most, that the award may be for a less important aspect of the program.

News That Glues

Television is a news hog, always hungry and looking for more stories. Without news, after all, there would be no news shows. News producers want to glue their audiences to the television screen and keep them tuned into their programs. So, they look constantly for stories that will do just that. Since certain subjects such as crime, natural disasters, popular entertainers, or controversial politicians usually draw lots of viewer interest, TV news people pay special attention to these subjects. Sometimes when a story is "hot," they will pay so much attention to it that there really is not anything more to say. But since it has been drawing viewers, they are reluctant to let it go. They begin looking for fresh angles to it, ways to wring just a little more from the story before they have to let it go.

For example, pretend that popular singer Johnny Angrythroat wins a Nobel Peace Prize for his work fighting poverty in Third World countries. Johnny is obviously big news for a day. In fact, by the end of the day, with all the network, cable, and local news coverage, the story has pretty much played out. Just about everything that could be said has been said. But since Johnny has lots of fans who are always ready to hear anything about him, the TV newscasters may start trying to stretch the story—maybe, for instance, by interviewing Johnny's hairstylist or the guy who designs Johnny's clothes. Is this news? It is on the news, so it must be . . . right? But maybe we should wonder what else might have happened that day that may have been a little more important than an interview with Johnny Angrythroat's hairstylist. Sure, the story only took a minute or so of airtime, but could that minute not have been better used to give more important information?

In the 1990s, Michael Jackson was an enormously popular singer and performer, until widely publicized scandals brought his career to a standstill. So in 2001, when Michael Jackson brought out his comeback album, his return was big news. TV news programs covered the album release. Then they covered preparations for a spectacular Michael Jackson Thirtieth Anniversary Tribute concert on September 7 in Madison Square Garden in New York. Next, they covered the concert itself. Finally, the next day, they covered what Elizabeth Taylor wore to the concert—along with coverage of appearances by Britney Spears (who sang with Michael), Whitney Houston, Liza Minnelli, Ray Charles, Cassandra Wilson, Gloria Estefan, James Ingram, and on and on. The story still played out in December when Liza Minnelli and TV producer David Gest married in New York—they had met at the Jackson concert in September.

This was all programming that played well. Michael Jackson has always been flashy and fun to watch. He has celebrity. He is entertaining. He has famous friends, such as Taylor, Spears, and the rest. He is notorious. There is also suspense in the story: Can Michael Jackson make good on his comeback? Will he ever regain his former fame and success? All this news was entertaining—but possibly not the most important news for such long, drawn-out coverage.

Celebrity news often boosts ratings for TV stations. Pictured here are Justin Timberlake of 'NSYNC and Britney Spears at her album release party in New York, November 6, 2001—before their romantic breakup, which received enormous media attention.

"News You Can Use"

In the great battle for viewers and ratings, television newscasts have turned to another trick to capture viewer attention and, as a result, the phrase "news you can use" has become a new buzzword. What is "news you can use"? For the most part this is just another way of describing what some newscasters refer to as "news lite," or "soft news" stories—stories about colorful local characters, celebrity interviews and gossip, and most frequent of all, health-related stories.

Typical of this kind of "reporting" was a "news" segment that appeared recently on Seattle television. With important real news stories breaking out all over the globe, the Seattle station used some of its valuable time to tell viewers all about toothbrushes. Among other facts, viewers learned that they should replace their toothbrush every three months and that the costs of brushes ranged from $1.89 to $5.00. They were also informed that a display of toothbrushes in an average market could take up a space six feet wide. The story concluded with advice to the viewer that, actually, the kind of toothbrush people use does not matter as much as how often they regularly brush their teeth.

As silly as this example might seem to be, health issues are always a concern with television viewers. So television news programmers take advantage of that interest by offering more and more health segments on their shows. The problem here is that health issues are often complicated. Given the limited time available on any individual newscast and the limited scientific knowledge of most viewers, many of these health segments are superficial stories about trendy or alternative health practices. These are generally practices, such as homeopathic medicine, herbal medicine, and so on, that most legitimate health practitioners stay away from.

Of course, sometimes health-related stories feature the latest scientific findings from reputable researchers. But even then, TV news programs are usually too short and too superficial to give viewers the helpful, in-depth information they need.

6

Thinking Critically About the News

1. **Look for the elements of storytelling in television news.** News programs are based on reality, but how closely does what you are watching reflect reality? Are the elements of a good story present? If so, maybe at least a little bit of skepticism is called for. Real life does not usually shape up into the elements of a good story. Usually someone has shaped, trimmed, and rearranged the facts. Maybe the presentation is only a *part* of the reality. (In fact, it is impossible to tell the *whole* story about anything in a few seconds or

89

even a few minutes.) Does the presentation fit in a story category, such as human interest, political, or crime and violence? Do you recognize character types? Is there a hero or heroine? Is there a victim who has never had a break? Is there a villain? Whose point of view does the story take?

As authors Neil Postman and Steve Powers point out in their book *How To Watch TV News*, the very structure of a television news broadcast is set up as a dramatic theater event. It begins with a musical opening, and the camera sweeps across a busy-looking dramatic set, where anchors and reporters seem to pause from their busy day to provide viewers with a news update. Lighting, makeup, carefully contrived costumes and hairstyles all contribute to the theatrical scene.[1]

2. **Compare how different media and different programs handle the same story.** How does the lead TV news story compare to the same story told by the same day's front-page newspaper headline? How does it compare with the story told by a print newsmagazine? How did different television news programs handle the story? This is an especially interesting exercise when a big story dominates the news. If Internet access is available, try taking a look at the same story as covered by newspapers and news agencies in other nations. How does the British Broadcasting Company (BBC) handle the story?

How about *The Times* of London? How does it look from Canada? Try some other countries, too. Are they all even covering the lead story featured on TV news? As one educator says, "If it is news, why do they not all cover the same stories, or cover them the same way?"[2]

3. **Look for the slant or bias of the story.** Is the presentation neutral? Or is it negative? Or positive? What kinds of words are used in telling the story? Are they loaded with antagonism? Or praise? Do they appeal to emotions? Look at the pictures used to illustrate the story. Do they convey a prejudice?

4. **Notice who sponsors the program or segment.** What does the type of sponsor show about the expected audience? Is the orientation toward family? Or toward investment-oriented professionals? Or toward teens? Or toward sports enthusiasts? Noticing the sponsor may give clues about the bias of the program. The program's bias will attract certain kinds of sponsors. Also, those sponsors may influence the program's contents and slant. Advertisers do have a lot of power. In 1997, the national media watch group FAIR (Fairness and Accuracy In Reporting) reported that David Horowitz, a consumer reporter for KCBS-TV in Los Angeles, had been fired after automobile advertisers complained to station management about his stories on car safety.[3]

Using a Bias and Baloney Detector

Critical thinking can supply the tools to look beyond the facade, or surface appearance, to see some of the complexities beneath it. By asking a few questions of oneself, one can begin to see patterns and sleights of hand. Here are a few more thoughts about how you can become better at recognizing signs of bias, hurried reporting, slant, spin, and glitz.

Word Games. Bias can happen intentionally or unintentionally. Television writers, reporters, and newsreaders are as human as the rest of us. One interesting and fun way to demonstrate how bias can color a news story is to choose another word or phrase for the words used by a television newsreader in a story. One person's "terrorist" may be someone else's "freedom fighter." An "angry mob" demonstrating outside the gates of a big corporation accused of polluting the environment might also be called "concerned citizens." The corporate spokesman answering their "complaints" (try "concerns") may not be "evasive." Instead, he may merely be "careful." His boss, the "corporate czar," may be simply "the president of the company," who may be described as a "wealthy" businessman or a "successful" one. What about that "community spokesman"? Or is he a "self-appointed leader"? Could his "angry" words be referred to as "passionate" instead? Were the protesters "unruly," or were they "demonstrative"? Did "violence erupt," or did "tempers become heated"?

Photo Finagle. Still working with the same imaginary newscast, let us take a look at how bias also creeps in with the video pictures that a television news director chooses to show. Are there more shots of protesters throwing rocks and breaking windows, or do most of the pictures that flash onto your television screen show helmeted policemen with shields clubbing young men and women? Do we see a protester going limp and passively allowing herself to be carried into the police wagon? Or does the camera lens focus on another—this one engaged in a frantic fist-flying battle?

Even the way that the cameraperson moved the camera can alter the presentation of the event. The pictures from the television camera help provide the event's atmosphere and convey an attitude. Is the camera movement slow and steady, moving around in a calm way as it captures the pictures, or does it jerk quickly, showing lots of fast shots, and changing angles abruptly from one shot to the next? Do we see an apparently orderly demonstration or one that seems disorderly?

Position Is Everything. In thinking about the effects of presentation, remember too that position in the time slot plays a key role in the audience's impression of the story's importance. Is it the lead story (the first one), showing that the news director feels that it is of prime importance? Or does it show up much later in the news show, maybe just before the sports or weather, indicating that it is of lesser importance? While it may be of great importance to the demonstrators and the organizers of the demonstration (after all, that is what demonstrations are for—to get noticed), it may be thought by the news director to be of lesser importance to the general public, and certainly the "corporate leaders" of the story will be relieved if it appears to be "played down." Where the newscast decides to place a particular story in its nightly news can determine how important the average viewer thinks the story is. A bias, either intentional or unintentional, in the choice of the story's placement by the news director can have great impact on what the viewer thinks about the story.

Another placement strategy is to place a story with high audience interest at the end of a program—along with lots of reminders, or teasers: "Later, we'll hear from local champion Sarah Hughes about her gold medal win," or "Spelunker saved in daring cave rescue. That story next." And, of course: "Stay tuned."

Voice Vote. Take note of the voice intonations and physical movements of the newsreader. How do they color the way the viewer thinks about the event? "Senator Smith disagrees with the president's plan to lower taxes," the newsreader informs us. Does she raise an eyebrow when she says this, smiling slightly and suggesting by her voice and body movements that we all know Senator Smith is an argumentative dissident and a bit flaky, besides? Or does he use solemn tones, looking steadily and seriously at the camera, suggesting that Senator Smith, representing us all, is once more holding up the voice of reason on our behalf?

Speaking of News

Be sure not to confuse talk show hosts with news reporters. Although Larry King, the host of the popular show *Larry King Live*, may appear to act like a reporter as he interviews his guests, it is important to remember that it is not news that he is after but answers that will entertain his audience. Often King and other talk show hosts will have people who are in the news as their guests—that is, someone who has recently figured in a major or controversial news story. Politicians involved in scandals, writers of controversial books, lawyers who have been involved in sensational trials all may at one time or another appear as guests on talk shows. It is important to remember that everyone who has been selected to appear on a talk show has, for reasons of his or her own, agreed to the appearance. Guests who appear on talk shows always have reasons for wanting the publicity. They believe that their appearance will benefit them in some way. They may be seeking to promote a book. They may be hoping to change the public's perception of them or someone they represent. They may be trying to convince the viewers that they have special talents or insights. There are many reasons why a guest may agree to appear on a popular talk show. But no one who agrees to spend twenty or thirty minutes or even more being questioned by a talk show host, members of the studio audience, or call-in viewers does so without believing that he or she will receive some kind of a benefit from such an appearance. This is understood by both the guest and the talk show host. The unspoken agreement is that the guest will receive his or her "benefit" while the host will receive "a good show." The questions the host asks the guest may be deep and probing. Often they may even seem to be attacks—for example, suggesting outright that many people do not believe that the guest is telling the truth about a particular subject. But always both the guest and the host are aware that if the host goes too far, that is, if he casts the guest in too bad a light, then the agreement will have been broken and the host may find it difficult to secure guests for future shows.

Despite the image, the Larry King Live *show is not a news program. Guests appear on the show to promote themselves or a cause. Shown here, Larry King meets with presidential candidate George W. Bush before the 2000 presidential election.*

The Retold Story

Another disturbing effect some TV newsmagazines have begun to use is the reenactment of news stories by actors who play out the roles of the original people involved in the stories when no original film of the event is available. This may be a reconstruction of the believed last few minutes of a missing woman as she walked down the streets of a waterfront shortly before she disappeared. Or it may be actors, with their faces carefully hidden, playing out the actions of an elaborate bank robbery.

Some newsmagazines actually specialize in reenacting of dynamic stories such as dramatic rescues. For these they use as many of the real participants as possible but employ actors to play the parts when the real participants are unavailable. The problem, of course, is that what the audience sees is not the actual event, but a reconstructed one, and that means one staged by a director and completely under the control of a director's decisions. From the choice of camera angles to the physical movements and the words of the actors, the event is staged to offer the most dramatic impact. Did one of the rescue team actually desperately utter the words "Man, I do not think that this guy is going to make it," at the time of the real rescue? Or did the director decide that these words should be added during the reconstruction to build up the worry and anticipation on the part of the viewing audience? Did the hapless victim really offer a weak but heroic smile as he was pulled from the wreckage of the collapsed building, or was that too added during the reconstruction to add a touch of warmth to the climax?

Opinion, Anyone?

Remember, it is not necessary to have an opinion on everything. Sometimes it is wiser to wait, observe, and gather more facts than to form an immediate opinion based upon limited information.

Even though it might be hard to believe in these days when everybody seems to have an opinion or an attitude about everything, it really is not always necessary to have an opinion. And it is certainly wise not to form one based on the limited information provided by a single television news show. Also, forming an opinion should be an individual process. Your opinion should be yours, not someone else's. An opinion is a reflection of the person holding it, and it should be formed with considerable care and only after careful thought and study. Even then, though, it is always important to be ready to change an opinion if new information comes to hand. It is only the very stubborn or the very ignorant person who is not prepared to change his or her mind upon the discovery of a new fact.

Epilogue

Overall, television news reporters do a good job. Most try to be unbiased and fair as they collect facts and report on them. Because their jobs are high profile, people are always talking about their work, retelling their news stories, commenting on their appearance, and reacting to TV news programming. News reporters also take a lot of personal risks, and what they do is often dangerous. Sometimes, they risk their lives just doing their jobs. A newspaper reporter named Daniel Pearl, who worked for the *Wall Street Journal*, was kidnapped in Pakistan in January 2002 and murdered for trying to collect facts for a news story. He was not a TV news journalist, but the same thing could happen to a reporter working for a TV network. These professionals deserve tremendous credit for doing an extremely difficult job—a job that is impossible to do perfectly day in and day out.

This book has looked at common shortcomings that can make television news reports less than perfect. Some warped presentation takes place because concessions are made to advertisers. Programming is designed to please advertising sponsors and the public alike. The motive is profit—to please the sponsors and the audience and make more money. There is nothing fundamentally wrong with that idea. In fact, this country's economy is built on the idea that making a profit is healthy. The problem lies in what kinds of decisions one makes in the process of making a profit—and what effects those decisions have on the quality of the news programs produced.

Would another system work better? Public broadcasting, such as the Public Broadcasting Service (PBS), which is owned by public supporters, makes concessions too, as discussed earlier in this book. They are just trying to gain success in a different way.

What about state-controlled broadcasting? Many countries have state-owned news stations, including Morocco, Italy, Madagascar, China, Iraq, Slovakia, and many others. However, state-controlled stations generally have a bias directed by the political party in power. If the government has a monopoly (controls all TV broadcasting) the impact on freedom of the press and freedom of information is devastating. During the Persian Gulf War, Iraq controlled all TV programming, and citizens of Iraq received the news from only one point of view—the government of Iraq's point of view. At least that was true until some citizens reportedly figured out ways they could receive the news from CNN.

In the United States, freedom of the press is a fundamental constitutional right. Of the options, the commercial and public television choices still serve that freedom best—or have the best hope of doing so. Competition always offers the possibility for variations. Control may change hands, sponsors come and go, but underneath it all, the ideal of freedom of the press remains.

Human nature may intervene, and so do the pressures of competition and the increasingly complex relationships between the news media and corporate America. Perhaps the ideal of fair, unbiased, in-depth news reporting can never really be achieved consistently, day in and day out. But the expectation of the ideal must remain, in the hearts of the newscasters and journalists—and especially in the hearts of the audience.

Beyond that, every member of the audience has three other important responsibilities: (1) to think critically, (2) to understand and recognize the pressures that shape the programming, and (3) to watch television news with a discriminating eye, an informed mind, and an unbiased, honest attitude.

To survive, a democracy must have an informed citizenry. Television is one of the major sources of information in today's world, and it is certain to remain so for a long time. However, exactly because it is so powerful, such an influential medium requires careful thought from those who use it. To do its job correctly, television news calls for constant and critical dialogue from all its viewers.

Chapter Notes

Chapter 1. Stay Tuned for the News

1. From a Media Studies Center survey by the University of Connecticut, conducted January 11–18, 1999, among 1,002 adults nationwide, <http://www.pollingreport.com/media.htm> (June 11, 2001).

2. Martin Mayer, *Making News* (Garden City, N.Y.: Doubleday & Co., Inc., 1987), p. 99.

3. James Glen Stovall, *Writing for the Mass Media, 4th Edition* (Boston: Allyn and Bacon, 1998), pp. 116–118.

4. *The Oxford Dictionary of Quotations* 1999, <http://www.xrefer.com/entry/247730> (May 16, 2002).

5. Steve Johnson, "How Low Can TV News Go?" *Columbia Journalism Review*, July/August 1997, <cjr.org/year/97/4/tvnews.asp> (August 27, 2002).

6. Ted Koppel, *Off Camera: Private Thoughts Made Public* (New York: Alfred A. Knopf, 2000), p. 217.

7. Ibid., p. 88.

8. "Code of Ethics and Professional Conduct, Radio-Television News Directors Association," September 14, 2000, <http://www.rtnda.org/ethics/coe.shtml> (October 29, 2001).

9. Ibid.

Chapter 2. Inside TV News

1. Rob Walker, "Anchor Steam: Why the Evening News Is Worse Than 'O'Reilly,'" *The New Republic Online*, May 10, 2002, <http://www.tnr.com/doc.mhtml?i=20020520&s=walker052002&c=1> (May 11, 2002).

2. Valerie Hyman, "The Producer's Challenge," *The Producer Book*, May 1996, <http://www.scripps. ohiou. edu/producer/thebook/chapter1.htm> (May 16, 2002).

3. Ibid.

4. Christine Craft, *An Anchorwoman's Story* (Santa Barbara, Calif.: Capra Press, 1986), p. 9.

5. Ibid.

Chapter 3. Who Is Running the Show?

1. Richard Campbell, *60 Minutes and the News: A Mythology for Middle America* (Chicago: University of Illinois Press, 1991), p. 2.

2. James Fallows, *Breaking the News: How the Media Undermine American Democracy* (New York: Vintage Books, 1996), p. 55.

3. John Powell, "What the Ratings Really Mean," May 25, 2000, <http://www.canoe.ca/SlamWrestlingEditorial/may25-powell. html> (November 18, 2001).

4. Neil Hickey, "Money Lust," *Columbia Journalism Review*, July/August 1998, <www.cjr.org/year/98/4/moneylust.asp> (August 27, 2002).

5. Ken Lindner, *Broadcasting Realities: Real-Life Issues and Insights for Broadcast Journalists, Aspiring Journalists, and Broadcasters* (Chicago: Bonus Books, Inc., 1999), pp. 14–15.

6. Ibid.

7. Dan Rather, with Mickey Herskowitz, *The Camera Never Blinks Twice: The Further Adventures of a Television Journalist* (New York: William Morrow and Co., 1994), pp. 335–336.

8. Neil Postman and Steve Powers, *How to Watch TV News* (New York: Penguin Books, 1992), pp. 5–6.

9. Ted Koppel, *Off Camera: Private Thoughts Made Public* (New York: Alfred A. Knopf, 2000), p. 64.

10. Postman and Powers, p. 48.

11. Neil Postman, *Amusing Ourselves to Death: Public Discourse in the Age of Show Business* (New York: Penguin Books, 1985), p. 105.

12. Steve Johnson, "How Low Can TV Go?" *Columbia Journalism Review*, July/August 1997, <cjr.org.year/97/4/tvnews.asp> (August 27, 2002).

13. Neil Hickey, "Money Lust," *Columbia Journalism Review*, July/August 1998, <http://www.cjr.org/year/98/4/moneylust4.asp> (August 27, 2002).

14. Lawrence K. Grossman, "Shilling for Prime Time," *Columbia Journalism Review*, September/October 2000, <www.crj.org/year/00/03/grossman.asp> (August 27, 2002).

15. Center for Media Literacy, "How to Detect Bias in the News," *Intermedia*, August 1, 1995, <http://www.cyberpod.com/cyberpod/media3.htm> (August 27, 2002).

16. Rob Walker, "Anchor Steam: Why the Evening News Is Worse Than 'O'Reilly,'" *The New Republic Online*, May 10, 2002, <http://www.tnr.com/docprint.mhtml?i=20020508&s=walker052002> (May 11, 2002).

Chapter 4. When Trust Is in Danger

1. *The National Enquirer*, May 18, 2002, <http://www.nationalenquirer.com> (May 18, 2002).

2. *Weekly World News*, February 26, 2001, <http://www.weeklyworldnews.com> (October 15, 2002).

3. *Weekly World News*, July 19, 2002, <http://www.weeklyworldnews.com> (October 15, 2002).

4. Ted Koppel, *Off Camera: Private Thoughts Made Public* (New York: Alfred A. Knopf, 2000), p. 258.

5. Ibid.

6. Richard Campbell, *60 Minutes and the News: A Mythology for Middle America* (Chicago: University of Illinois Press, 1991), p. 36.

7. Ibid.

8. Fallows, p. 186.

9. Koppel, p. 182.

Chapter 5. Some Tricks of the Trade

1. Christine Craft, *An Anchorwoman's Story* (Santa Barbara, Calif.: Capra Press, 1986).

2. James Fallows, *Breaking the News: How the Media Undermine American Democracy* (New York: Pantheon Books, 1996), pp. 57–58.

3. Ibid.

Chapter 6. Thinking Critically About the News

1. Neil Postman and Steve Powers, *How to Watch TV News* (New York: Penguin Books, 1992), pp. 108–109.

2. David Considine, "How to Analyze News: A Practical Framework for Teaching Students," *The National Telemedia Council, Media Awareness Network Web site*, <http://www.media-awareness.ca/eng/med/class/teamedia/htan.htm> (August 27, 2002).

3. Lawrence Soley, "The Power of the Press Has a Price: TV Reporters Talk about Advertiser Pressures," *Extra! The Magazine of FAIR* (Fairness and Accuracy in Reporting), July/August 1997, <http://www.fair.org/extra/9707/ad-survey.html> (May 18, 2002).

Glossary

advertising—A message paid for by the sponsor, or advertiser. Its purpose is to persuade viewers to buy the advertiser's product or accept the ideas in the message.

bias—Prejudice that impairs impartial judgment; one-sided view, often prompted by motivation to see things in a certain way.

code of ethics—Rules governing what is considered honest, fair, and acceptable in an industry or organization.

correspondent—A reporter who contributes news or commentary to a newspaper or television or radio station, often from a remote location.

documentary—An unscripted film reflecting real events.

FAIR (Fairness and Accuracy in Reporting)—A national media watch group.

feature story—A story that focuses on entertaining and informing but does not cover the breaking news of the day.

media—A means of mass communication, such as radio, television, newspaper, magazines, or the Internet.

newsmagazine–Television news shows that present in-depth feature stories rather than breaking news.

Nielsen ratings—An independent system rating the popularity of local and national television shows.

objective—Fair; not slanted in either direction.

propaganda—Ideas, facts, or allegations spread deliberately to further one's cause or to damage an opposing cause.

Public Broadcasting Service—A network established by Congress in 1967 primarily for educational programming. It is financed by the federal government, corporate sponsors, and contributions from individual viewers.

sensationalism—The practice of presenting news full of lurid detail to excite interest.

sponsor—A person or organization that pays for the cost of a TV or radio program in return for advertising time.

tabloid—A newspaper in small format that gives stories in condensed form—usually having an overstated, sensational style.

television production—The process of creating a television show; broadly, all the steps from idea, research, fact-gathering, and scriptwriting to taping, sound recording, and titles to videotape editing.

Further Reading

Gibson, Diane. *Television*. North Mankato, Minn.: Smart Apple Media, 1999.

Gourley, Catherine. *Media Wizards: A Behind-the-Scenes Look at Media Manipulation*. Brookfield, Conn.: Twenty-First Century Books, 1999.

Merbreier, Carter, and Linda C. Riley. *Television: What's Behind What You See*. New York: Farrar, Straus & Giroux, 1995.

Morgan, Sally, Catherine Chambers, and Pauline Lalor. *Behind Media Series: An Insider's Look at the Media Industries*. Chicago: Heinemann Library, 2001.

Petley, Julian. *Media: The Impact on Our Lives*. Orlando, Fla.: Raintree Steck-Vaughn, 2001.

Stay, Byron L. *Mass Media*. Farmington Hills, Mich.: Gale Group, 1999.

Internet Addresses

Center for Media Education
<http://www.cme.org>

Fairness and Accuracy in Reporting
<http://www.fair.org>

National Telemedia Council
<http://www.nationaltelemediacouncil.org>

Index

A

Abel, Alan, 61–64
advertisers, 37, 46, 72–73, 91, 100
advertising, 43, 72–73, 100
American Broadcasting Company (ABC), 37, 53
anchorperson, 27–28, 32, 34–35, 55, 77–80
awards, 82–83

B

bias, 23, 52, 54–55, 91, 92–94, 100
body language, 94, 97
Bogart, John B., 16
British Broadcasting Corporation (BBC), 38, 90
Broadcast News (movie), 70

C

cable networks, 37, 39, 84
Cable News Network (CNN), 40, 66–67, 101
camera angle, 54–55, 97
Campbell, Richard, 70
celebrities as news, 15, 18–19, 67, 85
Columbia Broadcasting System (CBS), 37, 53, 62, 73–74, 75
Columbia Journalism Review (CJR), 44, 49, 51
commercials, 30, 46
commercial television, 37, 45–46, 48–49, 76
Craft, Christine, 32, 34–35, 42, 78
critical thinking, 89–98, 101
Cronkite, Walter, 43–44, 62

D

Dateline NBC, 74–75
documentary, 24–25

E

elections, 15, 71, 72
entertainment
news as, 45, 51, 58–60
ethics in journalism, 22–23, 24

F

Fairness and Accuracy in Reporting (FAIR), 91
Fallows, James, 41, 80
field correspondent, 29–30
Fox News Channel, 40
Frank, Reuven, 49–51

G

Gingrich, Newt, 71–72
Gonzalez, Elián, 17
Grossman, Lawrence K., 51

H

Hatch, Orrin, 53–54
Hinckley, John, Jr., 64–65
Horowitz, David, 91
Hyman, Valerie, 31–32

I

Insider, The, 75
interpretive reporting, 25–26
interview, 24, 68–71

J

Jackson, Michael, 85
Jennings, Peter, 53–54

K

Kennedy, John F., 71, 73
King, Larry, 95–96
Koppel, Ted, 20–22, 47, 67–68, 76

L

lead story, 30, 54, 93
Leahy, Patrick, 53–54
Lindner, Ken, 45

M

MacNeil-Lehrer Report, The, 48
MacNeil, Robert, 48
Maurice, Dick, 64–66
MSNBC, 40

N

National Broadcasting
Company (NBC), 37, 42,
49, 51, 53, 62, 74–75
networks, 6, 36–40, 47, 53,
79
news
content of, 43, 46
definition, 12
director, 30, 54, 65,
92–93, 97
presentation, 8, 47–48,
89–94, 100
producer, 24, 30–32
story content, 43–46
news coverage, 7–8
bias in, 23, 52, 54–55,
91–93, 100
comparing, 90–91
newsmagazines, 40–41,
43–44, 51–52, 80,
97–98
newsworthiness, 15–19
Nielsen Media Research,
42–46
Nixon, Richard M., 71, 73

P

Pentagon, 6, 12, 16, 67
Postman, Neil, 46, 47, 90
Powers, Steve, 46, 47, 90
Public Broadcasting Service
(PBS), 37–38, 48, 51,
100
public television, 37, 48, 100

Q

Quayle, Dan, 72

R

Radio-Television News
Directors Association
(RTNDA)
Code of Ethics, 22–23, 24
Rand, Tamara, 64–66
Rather, Dan, 45–46, 73–74
ratings, 8, 32, 35, 42–46,
48, 49, 54, 66, 78, 87
Reagan, Ronald, 64–65
reenactments, 97–98
Reeve, Christopher, 72–73
reporter
on-location, 29–30, 32

sports, 28, 40, 78
weather, 28–29, 40, 78
Rocky Mountain Media
Watch, 49

S

satellite networks, 39
sensationalism, 56–57
September 11, 2001, 5–7,
12–13, 15
60 Minutes, 41, 59, 68, 70,
75
Society for Indecency to
Naked Animals (SINA),
61–62, 64
Spears, Britney, 18, 57, 85
sponsors, 8, 37, 38, 41,
45–46, 91, 100, 101
state-controlled TV, 100–101
storytelling, 89

T

tabloid news, 56–57
"Tailwind" report, 66–67
talk shows, 53, 64, 95–96
thinking critically, 89–98,
101
Time magazine, 67
TV news consultant, 32,
34–35
Twin Towers, 6, 12

U

University of Connecticut, 10,
12

V

video images
influence of, 54–55,
69–70, 93, 94, 97–98

W

Walker, Rob, 53–54
Wallace, Mike, 75
Walters, Barbara, 70
Warner Brothers Network
(WB), 43
World News Tonight, 53
World Trade Center, 6, 8, 12,
14, 16